Nery McMahon was born in 1956. She is Brazilian-born, but has lived in England for twenty-three years. She is a wife, a mother and grandmother. She has the belief that everybody deserves a good quality of life.

Dedicated to my loving husband and my dear friend, both brutally murdered in Bristol, UK on 3rd January 2003.

Nery McMahon

The Immigrant

Veronicas Story

AUSTIN MACAULEY PUBLISHERS™
LONDON * CAMBRIDGE * NEW YORK * SHARJAH

Copyright © Nery McMahon 2024

The right of Nery McMahon to be identified as author of this work has been asserted by the author in accordance with sections 77 and 78 of the Copyright, Designs and Patents Act 1988.

All rights reserved. No part of this publication may be reproduced, stored in a retrieval system, or transmitted in any form or by any means, electronic, mechanical, photocopying, recording, or otherwise, without the prior permission of the publishers.

Any person who commits any unauthorised act in relation to this publication may be liable to criminal prosecution and civil claims for damages.

This is a work of fiction. Names, characters, businesses, places, events, locales, and incidents are either the products of the author's imagination or used in a fictitious manner. Any resemblance to actual persons, living or dead, or actual events is purely coincidental.

A CIP catalogue record for this title is available from the British Library.

ISBN 9781035858774 (Paperback)
ISBN 9781035858798 (ePub e-book)
ISBN 9781035858781 (Audiobook)

www.austinmacauley.com

First Published 2024
Austin Macauley Publishers Ltd®
1 Canada Square
Canary Wharf
London
E14 5AA

A very big thank you to my husband, Glen, for his endless time spent re-writing and editing the revised English version.

No matter how many pieces your heart is broken in to, the world won't stop for you to fix it. Time is too precious and we can never bring that lost time back. So plant your own garden and decorate your soul instead of waiting for someone to bring you flowers, because the pain of regret is priceless.

Nery McMahon
07/05/2007

Preface

Based on her story, the author reflected and decided to dedicate this story to all women, children and adolescents who have been victims of physical, sexual and psychological abuse in their own homes. Just as Veronica fought to find freedom, so will you. Never give up the challenge.

The author's message calls for the youth and countless gangs of darkness that carry knives for taking lives, to lay down their weapons. Always remember that knives are to be used in the kitchen and machetes in the jungle, never to take away life. Taking the life of a fellow man does not belong to us. Therefore, always treat others as you would like to be treated and always show respect to be respected.

Chapter One

At the age of five, little miss Veronica lived on a rundown farm in Xuri, Espirito Santo in Brazil, together with her very large family; her mother, father, four sisters and three brothers. Her older brother Carlos and her father always woke up so much earlier than the rest of the family. Little miss Veronica would wake up with them as she loved to go to the fields to watch them work as they ploughed and harvested the greenery under the blazing hot sun. Carlos would always prepare a hearty breakfast for the three of them and at the crack of dawn at 5 o'clock, the work on the farm would begin.

One by one, her father would call on the comrades (as the workers that lived on the farm were known) to start their working day. They each lived in their separate houses, standing proudly along the dusty dirt track with their families. They each had their different work assignments; some in the paddocks and corrals, others in the muddy pigsties and half a dozen or so in the farms valleys and fields, together with Carlos and the adorable little girl, Veronica.

Carlos paid careful attention to his younger sister, as she was naïve and innocent as well as curious and mischievous. He always had her in eye shot, which wasn't too difficult as her favourite spot was the dirt covered, deep yellow tractor. She felt great joy when watching the land being ploughed in preparation for planting and the stirring aroma of the freshly churned earth fuelling her with the expectations of doing all again tomorrow.

She stood erect and alert during the planting phase, clinging firmly to the rusty iron mast of the tractor with one hand while using the other to gently toss corn and bean seeds in to the already prepared field. Her father Vitorinno had covered the monster sized farm vehicle with canvas, creating a homemade awning to protect her from the already warming sun that had quickly risen on the bright orange horizon. He felt compelled to do this since she consistently refused to remain at home with the rest of the family in the mornings.

Little miss Veronica dreaded the ten-thirty call, however, from Celina the housekeeper when she would come to take her back to the house for brunch. She always screamed loudly in protest but ended going anyway as with all children they soon become distracted by other things but also because she and her siblings had great respect for Celina as she had worked with the family for longer than eight years.

Upon arriving back home, her mother immediately made her bath as she did every day. After brunch, her mother suggested that she and her sister Flora go to their bedroom to play with their toys and dolls, insisting that if she didn't act like a girl, then she wouldn't be allowed to go to the field again. 'The fields are for the boys' she loved to say. 'Not for you, Nica,' as she affectionately called her.

Little miss Veronica had no interest nor the patience to play with dolls and all those little things that young girls are meant to enjoy. She played with her sister only for a short while before inviting her to play on the swing that hung lazily from the grand old avocado tree in the backyard. After swinging for a little while, they sneaked off to the pasture with their brother Dionisio, Dino, as he was known.

As they were going back in to the field without their mother Sara's permission, they could not take any of their riding equipment to the horse paddock on the far side of the dirt track, so they went riding bareback even though this was a taboo and specifically banned by their parents. She always rode with one of her older brothers, Dino's turn this time but it made no difference to her as long as she could feel the warm breeze in her hair and to feel as free as a bird. They loved to head down toward the Rio Jucu River as it flowed through the family's land.

On the partially muddy but grassy bank, they bathed the horses as they quenched their thirst before they all took a cool refreshing dip themselves. With plenty of somersaults and pirouettes, the return journey back home saw them checking the birds' nests build skilfully within the tree branches. They had marked the trees where the nests resided and lovingly but carefully looked after them, enjoying nature's beauty as the chicks fed greedily from their mother's beak.

They would also pick the local wild passion-fruit *pitanga* and *oraca* and knew exactly where to find them by the tempting sweet aromas that danced smoothly through the air. Little miss Veronica loved the passion-fruit flowers; the various exotic colours; their proud, elegant stance, with their enchanting beauty and addictive perfumes. It was Dino who always woke her from her moment of private contemplation.

"So are we going to pick some fruit or not?" he commented, holding his arms up aloft.

Her answer, as always, was a resounding 'yes' but this time she added, "Don't step on the flowers."

They scuttled around the fruit flowers laughing happily before delighting themselves by feasting on the sweet-smelling succulent natural fruit.

It was a few weeks later that little miss Veronica turned six-years-old and under the insistence of her parents, had to accompany her sister Ines to the province of Pinheiro where she taught young children at the local primary school. Ines returned home to the farm only three times a year; at Easter, during the June holidays and the long summer vacations.

However, it was agreed that in June, little miss Veronica would return home for her birthday. Ines gave her little sister a red velvet coat on her special day so that she could make the repetitive journey correctly and aptly dressed as it was a long and dusty ride in an ageing horse and cart. By the second week in August, all was ready and organised for her trip to Pinheiro.

When Sara saw her little angel ready to leave, a tear came to her eye. Flora also. Flora was three years older than her sister and they were very close. It would be the first time her close companion had ridden the horse and cart. Tall, proud, fully bloomed trees lined the dirt track on both sides, shielding the travellers from the midday sun.

Little miss Veronica admired the rugged but beautiful landscape as it slowly passed by. She jested with Ines not to ride through the fresh puddles from the rains of two days ago so as not to stain her lovely new coat with dirty brown water. Her young but curious mind constantly wondered what the place would be like at her final destination and more so about the people she would have to live with; about her living quarters in the house and how she would be received by the other and, if there would be children of her own age so that she could speak with equality and be fully understood.

She unconditionally loved Ines very much but felt uncomfortable in her presence occasionally because when she was born, Ines was already a grown woman. Because of work, she spent most of her time away from the family. She wondered and didn't understand why Flora hadn't come with her. She also considered that while she was away from home, it would no longer be necessary to go to the stall with her mother and, in order not to disobey her, have to drink warm milk directly from the cow's teats.

Her mother made her do this every day, claiming that it was good for her health and that she needed to put on some weight. Little miss Veronica refused to eat the meals that mother would cook and was beginning to show in her looks and demeanour.

Finally, she plucked up the courage and asked Ines if there were any children in the house where they were going.

"Yes, there are two young ladies and an eight-year-old boy but as you are already naughty enough, you won't get involved with him, will you," Ines insisted.

Little miss Veronica retorted, "I play with Dino and he's a boy as well."

Ines responded quickly, "Our brother is different. He takes care of you and this is not your brother, understand?"

"Why is he so different?" Veronica asked.

"Because he is and always will be when we are not with our family," Ines told her.

"Now, enough of this," she continued. "You *will* play only with girls of your own age at school. You will come with me to the school every morning. Mother says that you always wake up early, is that right?"

Little miss Veronica sulkily nodded her head. She looked down at her soil-stained shoes. "I want to eat some Kaki fruit."

"There is no Kaki in the basket. Have some guavas paste and curd cheese instead."

Once again, no words came from her mouth in reply, just a head shake lazily from side to side. "How much further to go?"

"An hour or so. No longer than that," Ines told her. "This cart is so uncomfortable to ride. My back aches!" She looked at her younger sister. "You look tired."

"I am," she agreed, gently rubbing her eyes. "When we arrive, I will rest for a while."

Ines nodded. "First, you must shower and eat dinner."

"I don't want dinner. I can eat tomorrow." Her interest in healthy eating was not improving.

"We'll see." It was not what Ines wanted to hear from her.

It was a further hour and a half before they finally arrived in Pinheiro province. Little miss Veronica was transfixed and hypnotised by the enormous difference between the countryside and the province. She had never been to a city before with so much activity; endless rows of shops; tall, chunky imposing buildings; a never ending stream of smelly and noisy motor vehicles and so many people that appeared to be wandering aimlessly on the street. It was both intimidating and intriguing. It made her feel strange; did she belong or was she an alien from the outback?

When she arrived at the house where she was staying with her sister, she was both delighted and in awe with its beauty and vastness but, to her disappointment, she would not be sleeping there, but in a rundown annex situated in the grounds.

"Why are we staying here?" she bluntly enquired.

Ines turned toward her. "Because all teachers that work at the school stay here for the duration of their employment," Ines explained. She took a little miss Veronica by the arm and guided her through the door. "Now young lady, let's take a bath, change those filthy clothes and then we'll unpack and put everything away." Little miss Veronica just stood there motionless. "Come then, let's get to it."

"You don't need to bathe me, Ines. I can do it myself."

"Hurry up then. I'll put everything away while to shower," Ines agreed.

After the bags were unpacked and the contents carefully put away, they ate a quickly prepared dinner; a light chicken and vegetable soup that Veronica barely touched.

Her first few nights away from home were a real struggle for her but Ines was very patient, supportive and affectionate with her. She could clearly sense the uneasiness that little miss Veronica was feeling.

On her first day at school with Ines, she was delighted with the school and with all the children playing together so happily. She had never seen so many in proximity, all so smartly dressed in their uniforms. Her fascination got the better of her as she wondered what she was going to do with so many girls that were all so different from her. All well attired, healthy and full of life. And me, thin and lanky. An odd girl that was so introverted with long, thick, braided hair. Dino once commented that she looked like a poorly dressed bamboo shoot.

Ines quickly noticed that she was distant and thoughtful with that recognisable sulky look. "What's wrong, Nica?" she asked.

"What am I going to do here?" Veronica grumbled. "I don't have a uniform like them so I can't study."

"You can't wear a uniform. Nor enrol. But you will be able to study." Ines removed a small brightly coloured case from her bag. "Here," she continued. "I bought this with us."

Little miss Veronica unzipped the case and peered inside. There saw a collection of pens, pencils and crayons. "These belong to Flora," she observed.

"That's right but Flora is enrolled in the second year at the ranch and you will go to school with me every day and learn as an assistant," Ines told her. "And when you enrol in the first year, you will be well on your way. You will have everything that you will ever need to begin your studies."

Four months passed and in December, Ines returned to the farm together with little miss Veronica.

Her father Vitorinno had decided that before Christmas, his wife Sara and the all the children would move to their home in Barra do Jucu, a small neighbouring village just twenty minutes away. With this move, the children would be able to attend school together. The family left for their short journey, leaving Vitorinno and Carlos alone on the farm but they always made time to visit them when work allowed them to.

Little miss Veronica soon turned seven years old and was subsequently enrolled in to the first grade at school.

It was just short of a year later that Sara suddenly and unexpectedly died of a stroke, leaving behind her eight-month-old daughter, Virginia, who was still breastfeeding. The tragic event disrupted the whole family and each member individually. Much sadness and pain was felt by all for a very long time.

Sara was an evangelical lady, a strong and contrite woman of god who spent much time in church with the children. The house garden, which was sizeable, was full of mourners. Family and friends and distant relatives travelled from the far reaches of the country in support of Vitorinno and the children, all sharing that tragic moment of sadness and Sara's favourite flower, the Dahlias, also feeling the pain or so it seemed.

Little miss Veronica clearly remembered the cold, lifeless atmosphere. After the doctor had gone, her eldest sister Zilar summoned the children to say their final goodbyes to their much loved mother amidst a flow of tears and grief. A spread was served shortly afterward, a mix of Mortadella, cheese and ham sandwiches and soft drinks for the children, all except little miss Veronica. Once again, she declined to eat anything, especially as she felt it was inappropriate on an occasion such as this.

Following the wake, Sara was buried in the Santa Ines cemetery in Vila Velha, a beautiful serene place that she loved for many years and often enjoyed visiting with the family. The funeral attracted some of the most important people from the area, including politicians and celebrities. The send-off was both beautiful and dignified and helped to restore some peace to the grieving hearts that were in attendance.

Three months after the emotional event, the married sisters requested a family visit together with Vitorinno, who had become increasingly withdrawn, bitter and sad with the family. During the visit, the elder sisters enquired about how he was treating the children. They asked their father for custody of their younger sisters who, without hesitation, agreed. It brought nothing but sadness to the youngsters, as they would all be separated and dispatched to different parts of the province.

Little miss Veronica witnessed these events with great anxiety, while at the same time, feeling a deep sense of loss and longing for her mother. However, she always kept her thoughts to herself and never spoke her mind because in the family, the children were expected to be seen and not heard. Any claim was seen to be insubordinate and disobedient.

Therefore, it was pointless explaining that the separation was painful for her and cruel or even expressing that they could not accept it. All that the children could do was to bite the bullet and await what may happen as a result of those awful choices until they were old enough to make changes for themselves. Only time would tell, in due course.

Chapter Two

At the age of eight, little miss Veronica went to live with her sister Ines in Campo Grande. There, she enrolled in the second grade at the local Baptist School.

Even at her still young age, Ines did not spare her from unwanted home chores, overloading her with housework and totally disregarding that fact that her studies must be priority. Despite having two daughters, Ines was constant in assigning her an extensive workload. Little miss Veronica would resentfully watch her two nieces' study and play together while she was 'working'.

When she explained to Ines that she had plenty of homework to do for tomorrow's lesson, she would simply say in a rude tone that she had plenty of time to study after she'd cleaned the kitchen after dinner. The chores had to be done completely to Ines criteria and satisfaction and any failure to do so would result in physical punishment. This would include hair pulls, face and body slaps, belts and pinches accompanied by loud vocal screams and derogatory words. This was not something that Ines did alone. She would actively encourage her husband to join her. Maybe she did this to alleviate some of the guilt that she may have felt.

Little miss Veronica no longer recognised her sister. The one who was always so loving and affectionate while her mother was alive.

Always feeling exhausted after school and with home and housework to be done, she never failed to complete the tasks, despite the aggressive objections of her older sister. She often dozed off over her schoolbooks, only to be subsequently and harshly awoken by a stinging neck pinch or a sharp glancing slap across her face; just a couple of examples of her sisters 'affection'.

Psychological mind games were part and parcel of her life now. Repairing old, faded and damaged clothes would always prioritise buying new ones. She felt violated. She felt used. She felt enslaved. She wore a multi-repaired school uniform that was too small. Her shoes were far too tight. Ines did not consider that she was a growing girl but still liked to beat her with the shoes, anyway. The limp she had acquired from her feet injuries was becoming more acute and painful. But she kept quiet. She said nothing despite that fact that her limp was plain for all to see. She did not want to instigate further abuse and beatings.

It was four years later, on Christmas day, that she received a beautiful blue dress, embroidered with beehive designs and a brand-new pair of black varnished shoes, from her brother-in-law. He told her that he presented the gifts to her for the festive occasion and also on merit, as there had never been a single complaint about her from the school and because he was aware of the hard graft had she endured at home.

He once made the observation that he had always stood by her. She believed that it was an insightful remark that still impacted her life to this day. It constantly reminded her that we often receive what we deserve and what we strive to achieve through our efforts and determination.

At the age of twelve, she was growing into a young lady. She studied for a further two years at the Estelida Dias College in Campo Grande and at fourteen, went to live with her sister Nadia in Praia do Sul. She was already in the third year of high school but at that time, she took a sabbatical from lessons to serve as a maid for her sister.

Nadia had four children and was expecting her fifth. She had a very problematic pregnancy. It was a year of great sorrow for little miss Veronica, who, despite having so much to do, couldn't accept not being allowed to attend school. But it was the same old story. They had decided without a care as to how she felt. Priority for them was that she was useful when needed.

Nadia's husband worked as a chef at a local and not very popular restaurant. He was a very heavy drinker and was persistently rude. He treated everyone with total destain with his abusive attitude and severe lack of respect. There was not an ounce of self-refinement to be found within him. As if little miss Veronica's suffering hadn't been enough, he aggressively forced her to carry water on her head to fill the three large water tanks that gave the house its regular supply.

It was arduous and very hard work for a youngster to undertake but, with grateful appreciation, her eldest niece helped her on occasions. It was a good forty-minute walk to the ice factory when they would collect it and a ninety-minute walk back. Her brother-in-law refused to help, even on his day off from work.

Three weeks before Veronica's fifteenth birthday, her older sister, who lived in Rio de Janeiro, unexpectedly arrived in Vitoria to visit Nadia and the family.

Upon seeing Veronica (too old now to be a little miss), she hugged her tightly for a moment before saying, "Young lady, you are growing up and so pretty too. But you look sad. You cannot offer me a smile. What's wrong?"

Veronica quickly glanced at the other faces present. "I haven't been to school for a very long time," she replied.

Her brother-in-law looked angrily at her statement. "You will never go to school while you live in my house," he spitefully insisted.

They had a short discussion about it, accomplishing or achieving any positives. There was going to be no change of heart or mind. Upon leaving, Zilar asked Nadia if Veronica and her niece could accompany her to the bus stop. She reluctantly agreed. On their way, Zilar made a promise to Veronica that she would not stay there for much longer and that upon her return to Rio, she would arrange with her older brother Carlos to get her out of there.

She again hugged her sister tightly. "It's a shame that our father has no idea of what is happening here," she told her.

Veronica shrugged her shoulders lazily. "He doesn't care about us," she observed. "The only interest he has is with his *new* family. My life is in god's hands now," she continued, "until I come of age."

"Just hold on for a little longer. Try to be strong. Carlos will come and take you from here," Zilar promised. "You will stay with me or Carlos. It is not safe for you here."

The bus came in to view from the far distance and eventually ground to a halt to a symphony of screeching, squeaky brakes. They said their goodbyes and the girls headed for home.

Upon arriving, their brother-in-law was filled with anger and fury. He grabbed Veronica violently by her hair and slapped her face with such force it caused her ear to ring and whine in protest and left a large red imprint. "What did she ask you?" he screamed at her. "Tell me if you don't want the living daylights beaten out of you."

Veronica's niece, together with the other children, screamed loudly and protested at his actions but he either deliberately ignored them or in his rage, just couldn't hear them. He pushed her to the floor and began to brutally kick her in the chest. Nadia tried to restrain him but was harshly ushered away by his elbow, causing her to fall backwards, hitting her head on the dinner table. Her head began to bleed. As Veronica lay motionless and in great pain on the kitchen floor, he turned on her niece, who, in terrible fear, had stepped back against the work tops.

"Tell me what she said," he continued the awful onslaught. Her niece, heavily shaking with fear, was crying uncontrollably.

She mumbled in a shaky voice, "Auntie Zilar said that Uncle Carlos will soon come for Auntie Nica and take her away from here." Somehow, she managed to get the words out.

Veronica's mouth and nose bled and, despite lying injured on the floor, gave her a few more kicks for good measure. He stopped and dropped down on to his hunches.

"Get up, bitch," he commanded. "Go and clean yourself up." He rose to his feet and stood erect. "I'll be waiting eagerly for your brother to come."

Veronica used the table to slowly pull herself to her feet. Tears streamed from her moist eyes. Despite the agonising pain, her legs were able to carry and support her weight. She looked down at Nadia. She was sitting on the floor, leaning against one of the table legs, holding her injured forehead. She said nothing as Veronica walked by her sheepishly, head bowed with her arms holding her chest. She slowly reached the bathroom, using the sink as support.

She trembled with despair at the image that confronted her in the mirror. Several facial injuries oozing blood and an eye that was already blackened and swollen. Blood dripped lazily from the corner of her mouth.

Using a face cloth, she gently and very carefully dabbed her injuries. 'Mother,' she prayed. 'Give me strength and help me with this suffering. What have I done to have to endure this? I feel like I am dying.'

Nadia walked in, still holding her injury. She looked dazed. She took Veronica by the hand and led her to the bedroom. "You need to change your clothes."

Each item of clothing that was removed revealed a bruise, scrape or another injury. Nadia softly applied warm salt and ointment to her mouth and nose. It stung harshly. "Lay down," she told her. "He won't hit you anymore. Don't be afraid." Nadia helped her on to the bed. "I'll make you some lemon balm," she continued. "You need to stop crying now. Your head hurts because you cry so much."

The lemon balm helped her to relax a little. Night time arrived, presented with a bright white full moon. She stayed alone in the bedroom that she shared with her niece. She didn't sleep. She was so overwhelmed that she couldn't think straight. Her emotions were so jumbled. She felt aimless, afraid, lost and defeated. How could she ever recover from this torment?

Veronica finally drifted off in the far reaches of the night but she didn't sleep. She just dozed like a cat resting on a branch in a tree. She awoke with a jolt, a sudden realisation of what had happened. But all was quiet, with everyone sleeping. She felt a chill despite the fact she lay beneath a blanket. She folded the blanket down and it was then that she saw her blood spotted underwear. *Oh god*, she thought to herself. *He has wounded me down there.*

She felt uncomfortable cramps and a stiffness in her groin. It wasn't an injury inflicted by her brother-in-law, though. In her naivety and her innocence, she was unaware that it was her first period.

Unsure of what to do, she straightened up in bed are rested her head on the cold concrete wall. She wouldn't be able to sleep any more, anyway. She would await daybreak and speak to Nadia about it when she awoke, even though she felt she couldn't totally trust her. She persevered with the unwanted cramps and chest pains and it wasn't long before dawn proudly arrived with thin streams of light piercing through the gap in the curtains.

A hazy silhouette appeared in her doorway and Nadia wished her a good morning.

Veronica returned the greeting before saying, "I hope you won't be upset with this but I need to go to the doctors," she explained. "I have an injury under my panties and it won't stop bleeding. I have felt ill most of the night."

Nadia sat on the edge of the bed and saw the deep red stain on her underwear. "It's OK," she said. "Go to the bathroom and clean yourself. Keep quiet and don't wake up anyone."

A minute later, Nadia joined her in the bathroom, holding a tampon in one hand and clean linen draped over the other. "You are not injured," she explained. "It is your menstruation saying its first hello to you. I've got some medicine for your period pain. It's an analgesic and will ease your chest pain as well." Nadia handed her a single pill to swallow. "You should stay in bed until you feel better. And stay away from the very one. Low profile until everything calms down."

Veronica, however, was burning up with fever (some time ago she was ill with fever for four days and was bedridden for eight). That evil pig of a brother-in-law had shown no remorse for his violent outburst; no apology; no polite inquiry. Not even a quick glance through the bedroom door to check on her. No one offered to take her to the doctors for a medical examination. They just left her to recover alone in her own time.

It was a full two weeks before it happened. She restarted her household chore routine, once again the ultimate slave of the house. Her brother-in-law was constantly on her case, belittling and degrading her with great satisfaction on his face. He taunted her with the words, 'when is your brother coming?' She fought hard to ignore him, offering silence in return, waiting patiently for her brother to come and take her away from there forever.

Every morning Nadia took her newborn to the health centre, leaving Veronica to do her expected slave duties and to care for the three-year-old boy who stayed at home while the others were at school.

She was tiding the dining room when she was startled by the loud, panicky voice of her brother-in-law. He should have been sleeping, as he had done a long night shift at work and always slept until mid-afternoon. "Come here, quickly," he called out.

With confusion in her mind, she raced upstairs to his room and, upon arriving, froze in complete shock. He was standing by the bed, totally naked and aroused. She tried to scream but he quickly grabbed her by the arm and pressed her tightly against the wall, gagging her painfully with his hand. He threw her on the bed and raped her violently and aggressively, with no malice or forethought. What lasted just a minute or two felt like an eternity, with Veronica unable to scream beyond her enforced entrapment.

After that scumbag coward had had his way with her, he simply said, "I trust you enjoyed your birthday present." He held her firmly to the bed as he produced a gun, secreted under his pillow and put it in her face, stroking the cold hard steel on her cheek. "Are you getting a good look at this?" he coldly continued. "This will be the last thing that you see before I kill you if you open your fat mouth to anyone. Nobody will believe you anyway but I'll still kill you." He removed his arm from her and pushed off the bed. She hit the floor with a loud thud. "Now get out of here, you slut and clean yourself up. And finish your cleaning before your sister gets back," he yelled. "Move it."

Tentatively but deliberately, she climbed to her feet, adjusting her torn blue and white shirt. She stood up straight, held her head high and slowly walked out. Despite her unnatural violation, she left the scene with some dignity. Perhaps a lifetime of physical and mental torture was now just the norm and to be expected but, beneath the surface, she was devastated with a destroyed, irreparable soul.

Chapter Three

With her clothes in tatters, she staggered slowly to the bathroom. Her panties, between her legs and thighs, were smeared with blood and semen. While stripping down, she peered at the small plastic bottle of bleach sitting beneath the sink. It stood out like a beacon, beckoning her, tempting her, asking her; insisting.

In deep, painful contemplation, she grabbed the bottle and removed the green coloured top, dropping it to the floor. She desperately needed to remove the emotional stains and scars imprinted on her body by that evil pig. She tipped the bottle forward and watched as the white liquid coated her skin. It stung harshly, like a hundred knives piercing her skin. She winced at the sharp pains, but the sensations felt good as they urged her to go further.

As the puddle of bleach on the tiled floor grew ever larger, Veronica put the bottleneck to her mouth and, without hesitation, tipped it forward. The lethal liquid flowed freely down her throat. It began to burn her with excruciating pain as it settled in her stomach. The bottle fell to the floor as she screamed in agony, her legs gave way as she collapsed to the floor, coming to rest beside the bottle that would set her free. The brother-in-law didn't come to her rescue. He lay on his bed, asleep in a drunken slumber. Veronica's eyes glazed over as their lids gently closed. She blacked out and slipped into unconsciousness.

Her neighbour, alerted by the loud, distressing screams, ran in to house and called out. She was answered with silence. One by one, she checked the rooms for signs of activity and eventually found Veronica slumped motionless on the floor. With a lifetime of experience, she didn't panic or stress.

After checking her over, she calmly but quickly descended the stairs and phoned for an ambulance. It subsequently arrived very quickly and sped Veronica off to the hospital. In all the drama that had unfolded, nobody had noticed that the three-year-old babe was still sleeping soundly upstairs, alone.

Veronica finally awoke after eight hours. Her stomach had been pumped out by the on-duty hospital doctor that had left her with niggling stomach pains and an awful headache. Her eyes opened to heavily blurred vision that took a moment to clear. She was greeted by the sight of Nadia, Ines and her eldest niece standing by the bed. Nadia sat on the bed beside her and took her hand in hers. She forced an unconvincing smile on her lips. "The doctor says you will be OK in time," Nadia explained. "How are you feeling?"

Veronica offered no reply, just a dark, distant stare.

A single solitary tear appeared in Nadia's eye. "Why?" she asked. "Why did you do this? Why did you try to kill yourself?" She nervously adjusted her position on the bed. "Don't you want to come with us to Rio? Ines came to pick you up. Why would you do such a thing? Tell us why you don't want to go."

Veronica glanced at Ines. "I didn't know that she was collecting me," she replied.

She was still feeling weak and dazed. "I was expecting Carlos to come." Her voice was shaky and slurred.

Ines took a step forward. "Yes, that's right," she said. "Carlos has arrived from Rio but he had to go to Sao Mateus first. When he is ready, he will stop at my house to pick you up and he will take you to Rio," Ines continued. "Nadia knew this all the time." She stood erect and folded her arms. "Why did you drink bleach?" She refused to allow Veronica to avoid the question. "You were very lucky that you dropped the bottle before drank too much."

The terrible image of the gun in her face entered her thoughts. It had caused her to pee herself and induce a minor panic attack. Once again, she offered no reply but began to cry again.

Ines looked sharply in to her eyes. "Don't ever do that again, young lady. Do you understand?" Her commanding moods always terrified her. "You will be fifteen years old tomorrow and you think of nothing but dying. You are safe now and out of danger." She paused for a moment, as if to compose herself. "The doctor said you'll be well enough to leave in a couple of days and this will all be over."

Veronica forced her eyes shut. "I'm sorry but I never want to set foot in that house ever again," she insisted. "Never, ever."

Nadia rose sharply from the bed. "I have done everything for you and this is how you repay me." She was clearly unhappy and upset. "This sounds like a severe lack of appreciation and gratitude."

Ines told her to stop crying and pull herself together. They would soon need to catch the bus to Campo Grande and would not be pleasant for a growing teenager to behave like a baby in the street or on the bus. She also suggested to Nadia not to worry about her sister's belongings as she could make use of some of her daughter's clothes as they were of a similar age.

Nadia agreed and with her daughter, departed the hospital and went home.

Ines remained at the hospital with Veronica until the time came for her discharge and, at the same time, try to persuade Veronica to divulge what had really happened. Her evasiveness was consistent and divulged nothing. She told Veronica to go and wash and, as the caring sister she was, helped brush her hair.

"Listen, you look much better now. You need to stop this silly whining." Ines' voice was calmer and more in control. "Everyone makes mistakes," she went on, "Heaven knows I have made mine. I am your sister and I am here to support you. You can trust me and tell me what's going on." Ines could not and should not let it go without explanation.

The evil images re-entered her head, not that they had disappeared. She shrugged her shoulders. "It's no one else's fault but dad's. He chose to put us all into strange houses to serve as servants with no pay, forcing us to work as slaves for food scraps not good enough for the dogs. Making us wear tatty old, second-hand clothes. And if that wasn't enough, having to live with constant abuse. It hurts us to the core." Her sadness and regret (and anger) was calmly controlled by clearly noticeable in her voice. "I just pray that my brothers are not suffering as I am so that our *father* will be happy with his new family."

"You shouldn't speak like that about your father," Ines retorted. "Despite his many faults, he is still your father. At just fifteen years old, you have no idea yet as to what life is all about."

"Whatever, but do you think it's fair that we left without a mother when we were all young and paid for our father's happiness with so much pain and suffering." Veronica slowly shook her head as she paused. "He doesn't even come to visit us. He doesn't even bring us school stationeries," Veronica continued. "Not even a cheap pair of socks, let alone his love."

"That's enough, Nica," Ines quickly replied. Did she really have the right to defend those actions from such a man? She pointed her index finger towards her face. "You have no comprehension on suffering," Ines paused before lowering her hand. "Come on, let's go. I'll treat you to some lemonade before we catch the bus home."

They halted at the nurses' station reception for Ines to sign the discharge papers, descended the flight of stairs on their left and exited the building. From that moment on, Veronica remained silent as she drank her ice-cold drink. Her sister offered her some lunch but she declined.

On the bus home, her silence continued but her fatigued mind was in constant turmoil over her evil brother-in-law. He was going to get away with what he'd done to the defenceless, innocent fifteen-year-old girl. She was desperate to tell someone, Carlos perhaps, but understood it could do more harm than good. She tried to convince herself that it would be better to wait for divine intervention to arrive someday soon.

With midnight not too far away, Veronica enquired as to where she would sleep. Ines told her that she could have her bed and she'd sleep on the couch. The following day, she had a rare but wonderful moment of happiness when she saw her brother, who had finally arrived from Sao Mateus. She excitedly ran to him and gave him a long, light hug. Carlos looked at her and smiled. "It's you," he commented happily. "It's really you. You are all grown up." He took her by the hand as they began to amble to nowhere in particular. "Nica, we are leaving for Rio today. Do you have all of your things packed?"

Veronica looked down and the dry, dusty ground. "I have nothing to take," she simply said.

"My wife has sent you a change of clothes as a gift. I'll go and get the bag from my truck for you," Carlos indicated. "Don't worry," he continued. "I'll buy you whatever you want and need later. I have arranged for you to stay with Zilar, since she is already with Virginia and Flora. She and her husband are more than happy with this arrangement and are looking forward to seeing you."

They arrived at the titanic sized lorry and he opened the passenger side door, removing a large plastic bag. He handed it to Veronica. "I will help you with all of your expenses and we'll go shopping for more clothes and some new shoes when we get you settled in Rio."

She opened the bag and peered inside. She was greeted with the sight of a pretty blue blouse, together with a pair of denim pants. A part smile appeared on her face as she had never worn such lovely clothes before, just dishevelled skirts and moth-eaten t-shirts. They were a perfect fit.

By night fall, they were well on their way on their long journey. Carlos preferred the night drive with little or no traffic. They talked and reminisced above the tunes playing from the radio, of the wonderful times and memories from the olden days in the countryside. She was so eager and excited to get to Rio to see her sisters. Carlos could not imagine that her joy was so significant. He drove that beast of a lorry for six hours without a stop for refreshments but fatigue finally got the better of him. He pulled in to a roadside services and carefully parked up.

He turned to Veronica. "We will need to make a stop in Campos as I need to collect a load to take to Bonsucesso. It's just some delivery I have to do."

Veronica had no idea what place he was talking about. She didn't care either. She just wanted to get to Rio to be with her two sisters, Virginia and Flora. After a quick snack, drink and bathroom break, they continued on their journey into the early morning. They eventually arrived in Campos where a fork-lift truck loaded a number of shrink-wrapped pallets on to his trailer, while the driver and passenger refreshed themselves with delicious bread and cheese with coffee and milk.

With the trailer fully loaded and meals devoured, they continued on the final part of the journey. "Not long to go now," Carlos told her. "We'll be at Zilar's house in a couple of hours."

Veronica dozed off to the soothing sounds of the radio, the spacious, comfortable cab embracing her like a mother to her baby. She slept soundly and eventually awoke to a day that had already dawned that was sunny, warm and beautiful.

"How much further to go?" she asked after completing her morning yawn.

Carlos turned his head to look at her. "We've arrived, Nica." He pointed his finger beyond the vast windscreen. "It's the next street. Just there."

She followed the direction of his finger and simply said, "What a lovely place. Such beautiful houses and tree-lined streets. I love it."

Veronica smiled. With a long hiss of the air brakes, the truck came to a halt adjacent to a house with a high wall and a large navy-blue iron gate. They disembarked, opened the squeaky gate and walked toward the door, through a beautiful, colourful and well-maintained garden.

Zilar opened the large wooden door and immediately hugged her brother. She called to the girls from inside the house, "Come see who has arrived." There was clear excitement in her voice.

It was Flora that appeared first, with Virginia behind her. Veronica was stunned at how much Flora had changed. At eighteen, she was now a grown woman with a full figure, beautifully styled hair and an outfit that would grace any magazine cover.

With a cute smile, Virginia acknowledged Veronica's arrival. Veronica reciprocated. She noticed how tall Virginia had become, despite that fact that she was just twelve years old. Zilar invited them in and immediately gestured them to the pre-prepared breakfast table. They all sat down and tucked in to a feast of toast and jam, cheese and crackers, breakfast cereal and a choice of orange juice or coffee.

Carlos sipped his hot coffee and looked at Veronica across the table. "So, you will be able to go back to school now." He set the coffee cup snugly on to its saucer. "We have already arranged one for you. All the paperwork is complete. But you must behave yourself here because it is very different from Vitoria. The boys here in the city are extremely extroverted, so be careful. Always listen to what Zilar tells you. From this day, she will be your mother so pay heed to all of her advice. For your own sake, do not deviate."

Carlos' advice was sound and important. "Whenever necessary, Zilar can call me if you need help or assistance." He raised his coffee cup again. "I am always here to help my family," he continued. "I will always be around but I have my own family to support. And my work. I don't want to see you in any trouble. I can't be here all the time."

Carlos shifted wearily in his chair. "You can visit me with Flora anytime you want to. She knows the way but always ask Zilar or her husband first." He rose from his seat with a stretch and a yawn. "I need some rest before I go home. Zilar, can you wake me around midday?"

She nodded in approval. "Go rest with god," she said. "I'll wake you up."

Carlos disappeared through the kitchen door and a moment later, a bedroom door closed.

Two months later saw the arrival of Veronica's school exams at the highly regarded school run by nuns in the region. If lady luck was watching over her and guiding her pen, then a pass would allow her to enter the first year of teacher training. A failure, which was not an option for her and the family, would mean another year at high school.

Dedicated to success, she studied hard with endless days and weeks in her bedroom, sacrificing any social life she may have had an interest in. The difficult and enduring work paid off as she passed all of her exams with distinction, to the delight and pride of everyone around her.

With great excitement, she began the training course that would take three years of dedication and devotion. Upon the successful completion of the course, her options would widen significantly but she had her eye on only one; to teach children in primary school. After many years of contemplation and inspiration, her dream would have come to fruition.

For the first time in her life, Veronica felt she finally belonged, had a purpose in her life and make her family genuinely proud of her. A beautiful smile came to her lips that, for the first time, wasn't forced nor faked.

Chapter Four

The entire family was over the moon for Veronica. Ecstatic. She had successfully studied at a prestigious school, providing her with full professional training in both home and social skills; childcare, cooking, sewing, social etiquette, knitting, crochet and embroidery, just to name a few. She felt blessed with her opportunity to devote herself to her studies.

At school, she had made good friends with two girls that were just as dedicated as she was. Regina, who was originally from Sao Paulo, had invited her to spend the holidays with her at her house. Veronica was fast approaching the age of seventeen and was becoming more independent, growing into a woman. Zilar knew Regina very well, as it was a common event for her to spend time in her house after school, studying with Veronica.

The two families met one evening during the December holidays so as to arrange and organise the final details for Veronica's stay in Sao Paulo with Regina. It was a meeting that was short and sweet as both families were happy with what was agreed and Veronica was soon on her way.

Despite the fact that she arrived late, the two girls were eventually met at the bus station by Regina's mother, who promptly took them to her house. Veronica quickly noticed that the relationship between mother and her daughter was a little odd; not what you'd expect. There was limited conversation between them and Regina was happy to always walk behind her.

Regina excitedly took Veronica's hand and led the way to her bedroom. "We will sleep here in my room together," she explained with a cheeky smile on her lips. "Mum was happy to squeeze another bed in here. It doesn't leave much space but at least we can do stuff together."

"I don't want to be any bother to you, mum," Veronica retorted.

"It's no bother, really." Regina sat heavily on her bed and stretched out her legs. "Mum likes it when I have friends to stay. It gives her some company. She gets lonely sometimes." Regina appeared sad.

With the luggage unpacked and everything in its place, Regina opened the top drawer of a chest that stood beside her bed. Veronica sat next to her as she removed various items, some jewellery together with make-up items, personal belongings that were both pretty and desirable, items that Veronica had never had the pleasure to own in her younger years. But it didn't concern her, despite their beauty.

She was now treated as a young lady with respect and dignity. She had decent clothes, like all the other girls, bought or made for her. She was very proud of her leisurewear. She had a watch and some costume jewellery. But she didn't care for it much. She was happy and fully content with the simple clothes that she owned; her comfortable pants, t-shirts and sneakers. After scanning her friends' items, she complimented her on her personal stuff.

Dinner was being prepared in the kitchen as its smell drifted lazily through the house, stimulating Veronica's senses. They both ambled in to the living room where Regina's mother asked them to set the dinner table. Veronica could clearly sense the uncomfortable atmosphere that stood before her like an unwanted guest at a wedding. She did not question it but as always, remained silent as she had learnt to do in her youth.

After dinner was taken, Regina's mother arose from the table and disappeared from the living room, not to been seen again for the rest of the evening. The dirty dishes were left for the girls to clean and dry before tidying the kitchen. After the chores were completed, they watched television for a short while before retiring to the bedroom.

Regina sat on her bed before removing her slippers. She swung her legs on to the bed and sat up, coming to rest on the small black bed head. She looked at Veronica, who was studying a magazine cover. "I'll tell you what is wrong with my mum provided you don't mention it to her nor tell anyone,"She said.

Veronica placed the magazine carefully on the bed and looked up. "OK."

Regina adjusted slightly, as if attempting to get more comfortable. "Promise me."

She nodded. "I promise."

There was a short pause as if she was composing herself. "My mum drinks a lot." She seemed embarrassed as she diverted her eyes to her wiggling toes sitting snugly within her white socks. "Yes, she is an alcoholic. She'll be drinking now in her room. She is heartbroken. She is sad and very unhappy," Regina explained.

"My dad died when I was eight years old and she has never recovered from it. She is in constant pain and turmoil, eight years after this happened." She paused again, taking a deep breath. "I don't suffer much now," she continued. "I don't really remember him much. All I have is an old photograph. That's all." She passed the beautifully framed picture to Veronica, taken from the chest of drawers. "That's why she sent me far away to another state to do my studies. She was so psychologically messed up that she was unable to look after me."

Veronica returned the frame to her and was replaced in its original position. She re-adjusted it, now satisfied with where it sat. "So there you are, Veronica. Now you know everything," she sighed. "Don't tell anyone and don't mention it to her, either. I'm trusting you with this. Be patient with her. She is moody and unpredictable, but she doesn't mean any harm."

"I know exactly how you feel," Veronica explained with equal sorrow. "I lost my mother when I was very young as well. I have experienced many bad times since then and still feel that awful loss. But look," she continued, sitting more erect on her bed. "We have come to Sao Paulo to hang out and have fun. I don't think it is appropriate to speak of such things now."

Regina nodded her head in agreement. "So tomorrow I will introduce you to some of my friends and we'll all go somewhere together. Don't worry, we'll have a lovely time here."

That night, they both slept like logs, through to 9 o'clock. After breakfast and some play time in the backyard, Regina took her to the Equestrian club. It was just a short walk from Regina's house as she lived on the new estate in Brooklin Paulista.

Veronica was both ecstatic and delighted at experiencing such a joyful moment with her friend. "This is so wonderful," she told Regina. "Just fabulous. I have never been to horse trials before. We have horses on the farm back home but they are mainly working horses and we can't ride them very often." She shook her head once again in disbelief, in complete collaboration with a huge smile.

"You haven't seen anything yet," Regina replied excitedly. "In the evenings, we will sometimes go to a bar with live music in Itaim Bibi. That always promises a lovely evening out."

Veronica looked somewhat surprised and a little shocked. "Your mother allows you to go out in the evening on your own?" she questioned.

"What do you mean, Veronica? I am almost eighteen years old. I often go out with my friends, especially when they meet me from home. Sometimes, they escort me back as well or I will catch a taxi." Regina wondered why she had to explain this to her. Maybe she has led a sheltered life, she thought. "Anyway," she went on, placing a hand on her shoulder. "Don't be alarmed or even scared if I get a little crazy on an evening out. It's just my way of having some fun."

There was no time for Veronica to retort as they were approached by two girls and a boy. Regina quickly introduced her high school friends to her. They said their hello's but Veronica, as always, remained quiet and discreet but observant.

The young boy quickly looked Veronica up and down with steely eyes and smiled, showing off his badly maintained teeth. "Wow, what a cutie," he said with a cheeky grin. "Do I have a chance?"

Regina sharply stepped in to his line of vision. "This is Nica but you get to call her Veronica. She is on vacation at my house so just back off, OK."

He held his hands up in both submissions but also in protest without saying a word and took a step back. Regina rolled her eyes before taking her girl friend's hand in an invitation for them to walk and explore. It soon became clear to Veronica that her good friend was very popular in town, as was her mother. Many attendees at the club either smiled at her or offered a pleasant verbal greeting, some enquiring as to how her mother was.

It wasn't long in their brisk stroll that they found themselves passing the riding club's lavish restaurant, an impressive, grand looking building with beautifully made bamboo dinner tables sitting on its patio. They all elected to take lunch, sitting at a table that was shaded by a brightly coloured umbrella. It was sandwiches all round with a cool, refreshing drink, all except Veronica. She once again declined to eat. It was the drink that only interested her.

After finishing her ham and cheese toastie, Regina sipped her coke and placed its glass carefully on the emptied plate. She looked across the table at Veronica, who was looking at her empty glass. "Wakey, wakey, Nica," she said in a loud, brash voice. "You doing OK there? You seem miles away. Where are you?"

She offered no reply as she had done so many times before in the past but offered only an unconvincing, limp smile.

"We should be going soon," Regina continued, resigned to the fact that no answer was forthcoming. "I have booked us an appointment at the local hairdressers at 2 o'clock this afternoon. We need to look our beautiful best for tonight as, in this town, the competition is significant. Once the sun sets, the boys come cruising!"

Veronica looked up in surprise. "What do you mean?" she asked.

"Her girl, lighten up." It was one of Regina's friends, offering her the unwanted and needless advice. Her sarcasm left a grinding feeling down her spine, as if someone were scratching a blackboard with their fingernails. It made her shiver. "We always go scouting for boys," came the same grinding voice. "Except in this town, the girls are the predators, and the boys are the prey."

"I'm not going to hunt for boys." Veronica's defensive position was clear to all. "I just want to have some fun with my friends."

"You're kidding, right?" The grinding resumed. "You'll be a major catch tonight. There are plenty of suitors and you don't even look your best yet."

"I have no interest in doing that." Veronica appeared hesitant, even scared. "I have no intention to date and I have no interest whatsoever, in a boyfriend."

Regina finished her drink and placed it heavily on the bamboo table with a dull thud. "What boyfriend, Nica?" she asked sharply. "Who wants a boyfriend? Don't take everything so seriously. Try to enjoy life while you're still young. After all, we are on vacation, are we not?"

Her patience seemed to be wearing a little thin. "Let me tell you something, right. I am sick and tired of those goody-two-shoes, stuck up nuns ordering me around and teaching me stuff that is pointless and useless. Stuff that will have no impact on my future. My future is going to be music. I want to be a musician, whether my family likes it or not.

"In a year's time, I will graduate with my degree in teaching and when that happens, I will throw it in the bin. I don't want to be a teacher. It will be very difficult to qualify as a musician and it's a long hard road, but my father left me enough money for me to try. And try, I will, with or without the support of my mother." Regina paused for a moment, expecting a comment from someone that never arrived. She shook her head. "It's as simple as that."

Veronica listened intently but quietly. She drew her own conclusions.

They spent close to two hours in the beauty salon, being pampered and waited upon by the beauticians and arriving home shortly before 5 o'clock after taking a slow and deliberate walk along the high street. For Regina, this was a time to tease the boys passing by, with the occasional beep of a car horn as it sped past. She loved the attention from the street guys. It made her feel good inside and artificially special. Veronica, on the other hand, felt nothing but embarrassment, hoping to be swallowed up by a deep black hole in the ground.

There were a number of messages from friends awaiting on their return. Regina subsequently returned the phone calls, explaining that she would be in Itaim for the evening. The three girls left the house at 9 o'clock and climbed in to a waiting car driven by a fourth friend. They all looked beautiful in their specialised make-up and evening attire; short skirts, thin, colourful designer blouses complimented with high heel shoes. As Regina had commented earlier, 'OK, girls, we're ready to rock.'

Arriving in Itaim, the car slowed and halted in front of a large, beautiful house to collect another friend of Regina's. Their first stop in the town centre was a fancy, up market bar with designer decor and retro, unique furnishings. The music penetrated the building, filling the tree-lined, busy streets with muffled baselines. The bar was only partially full of clientele seeking a good time; many drinking spirits in full measures while others shooting up drugs in hidden dark corners, away from prying eyes.

It took a moment for Veronica's eyes to adjust to the dim lighting, exposing an electric atmosphere of fire and ice. Her heart thumped rhythmically as her curiosity raced at the sights that stood before her. She had never experienced such emotions There were still many empty tables available as Regina guided her friends to one that was sitting close to the bar. There were four more girls already occupying it as they approached, more friends of their host!

They all sat down together except Regina, who was removing some money from her purse. "I'll get the first round of drinks in," she offered. "As I am your host. What would you like, Nica?"

"Just a diet coke for me, thanks. I don't drink anything else."

Regina smiled and shook her head. "Coke," she exclaimed. "Oh no, not a chance. If you want coke, then you'd better go to the children's party down the road. In here, we drink alcohol and lots of it."

The rest of the group shared a snigger and a laugh together. Regina looked at them in approval. "I know what you all drink but for Nica, I know exactly what she'd like."

It took just a few minutes for the drinks to arrive, presented on a stylish silver tray carried by the waitress. Regina handed Nica her full glass, who immediately put it to her lips. She hesitantly sipped it but quickly took another as her curiosity was satisfied and confidence increased. She savoured its rugged, sharp taste, briefly burning her throat as she swallowed. It tasted good and made her feel warm inside. She set the glass gently down on the table. "What the hell is this?" she asked.

Regina had half a smile on her face, almost a smirk. "It's a gin and tonic," she replied. "I knew you'd like it. Make you feel good, does it?"

There was no reply, as Veronica was already drinking more.

A young man appeared from within a small crowd and slowly approached the table, standing next to Veronica. He invited her to dance and before accepting, she nervously looked at the faces sitting at the table. What felt like an eternity was in fact just a few minutes and was a time for them all to leave and move on to the Flamingo disco.

Marcos asked for her phone number but told him that she was only in Itaim for a short time before returning home. He accepted her explanation and gave her his phone number instead, writing it on a one real monetary note. She rolled the note up and placed it in the top pocket of her blouse. With a smile, she said her goodbyes.

They all enjoyed the rest of their evening intensely. Veronica's thoughts drifted to Marcos during the evening a number of times but she wasn't sure why. During her stay with Regina, she had been invited out by a few guys but always declined as she had no interest nor inclination to go. Regina questioned it by asking, 'Are you really going to be alone for the whole of your vacation.'

It was a very simple reply for Veronica, 'But I'm not alone, am I? I have you. Anyway, what's the point? We go back to school soon and to tell you the truth, I don't know how to hang out with boys like you do. I feel embarrassed and just make a fool of myself.'

It wasn't long after their return to Rio, perhaps a couple of weeks, that Veronica's quiet and peaceful day was rudely interrupted by the screaming voice of Flora. She was clearly angry about something but could not understand what she was shouting about from across the backyard.

Flora halted ten metres from Veronica, still shouting loudly. "You have a phone call," she yelled, unaware that she was drawing the attention of passers-by on the dirt track. "He calls himself Marcos. Who the hell is he?"

Veronica began to jog towards the house. As she passed Flora, she said, "It's just someone I met on vacation."

She picked up the phone receiver that was swinging lazily against the wall. Flora entered the house and stood within earshot of her conversation, listening intently from the kitchen. It was a relatively short chat which was just as well, as Flora had heard enough. Her face was flushed and her eyes could not hide her anger.

"So who the hell is this guy?" Her voice was so loud it was as if she were talking to her from a mile away. Before Veronica could answer, she continued her outburst. "And why is he calling here? From what I could tell, it seems that you are in love with this guy." She momentarily paused in an attempt to compose calm herself. She folded her arms against her chest. "You want to tell me what's going on?"

"Thank you for turning down your voice volume," Veronica said sarcastically. "Right now, I have a lot to do." She began to back up towards the back door. "When I am finished, we'll go for a walk in the paddock. And yes, I have something to tell you."

Flora waited patiently for some three hours before she had completed her chores. She felt as though Veronica was deliberately taking her time just to frustrate her or was it just her angry imagination? They ambled to the paddock and sat on a lush patch of thick green grass. Flora seemed to be calmer or was it just a disguise? Veronica sat with her legs stretched out, resting on her hands.

"I don't really know what I feel but I find myself thinking of Marcos a lot. I guess I like him yes but why he on my mind is so much," Veronica told her. "Also, I could not invite him here to meet everyone because I have a serious problem that still haunts me even today."

Flora rolled her eyes and shook her head. "For god's sake. What is it? What's the problem that's making you so grumpy?"

Veronica looked away and up toward the mid-afternoon sun that was hiding within a maze of branches in the distant trees. She could not bear to look in to her own sister's eyes. "I am so ashamed of myself, telling you this," she said in a quiet voice. "I could not defend myself. He was too strong. I had no way." A tear appeared from her eye and lazily ran down her cheek.

"What are you talking about?" Flora's patience was running low.

It was not an easy story to tell, especially with the vision of the gun barrel pointing at her face. She took her time, pausing occasionally for composure and to summon what little courage she could muster as she recalled the hideous, terrifying moments of her assault. She stuttered uncontrollably as she forced the words out, with her heart beating like a repetitive, rhythmic drum. It felt just as horrific, reliving the ordeal, this time through words.

After the short, uncomfortable silence, Flora touched her arm gently. "Oh, I am so sorry, Veronica," she said. There was a sense of *Déjà vu* in her voice. "So that's why you tried to take your own life?"

Once again, Veronica did not offer an answer but the tears now streaming from her eyes, said it all. "My dear, innocent little sister," Flora continued. "He tried to do it to me as well, a long time ago. But I was lucky. He was interrupted by Nadia coming home."

The awful details of the assault were still clearly implanted in her mind but the pain had receded. "He also threatened me with death if I spoke out about it, but I never saw the gun. It must have been just terrifying for you." She paused as she attempted to shoo away an irritating fly buzzing about her head. The fly vanished.

"The reason I never said anything was purely because I didn't want to cause any rifts between the family. I'm not scared of him and never will be. But this situation is different. You were underage, just a child and he deliberately took advantage of your youth. That is not acceptable." Flora once again paused but this time because she was hesitant about her next statement. She took a long, deep breath. "You must tell Carlos and Zilar what happened."

Veronica's reaction was immediate and decisive, with a sharp shake of her head. "No way. No chance," she insisted. "Carlos would go to Vitoria and skin him alive. He'd ruin his life and Zilar's as well."

She wiped at her tears with the back of her hand. "Think about it for a moment, Flora. Carlos has a family and he already does so much for us. He has no obligation to get involved. If we tell dad, it will make it all the worse and he won't do anything about it, anyway. He doesn't care about us any longer, only his new family, so the evil pig will go unpunished forever. And there's Nadia as well. She wouldn't believe it, any of it. She always defends that monster and always has. What would Nadia do if she found out what a sick husband she has?"

Veronica adjusted her position on the grass, raising from her hands and placing them on her knees. "I am left in a terrible dilemma. What do I tell Marcos if he comes here to see me and we start dating? What do I say to him? Do I keep it a secret and withhold it all?"

Flora rose to her feet and carelessly brushed away blades of grass from her skirt. She held out her hand to help Veronica up from the greenery, who straightened her dishevelled attire. Flora did not like the conclusion of their conversation but what her younger sister had said did make sense, even if it was wrong.

"You have no dilemma right now, Nica," she promised, letting go of her hand. "You are not even officially dating, are you? And don't even consider the possibility of marriage because it's far too soon for all that." They both began to walk slowly towards the house. "And as for what happened to you, only time can repair and allow you justice. Put your trust in God, he will bring you retribution when he is ready."

She took her hand and began to swing their arms in perfect synchronicity. "As for the visit of Marcos, let's talk to the family and see if we can arrange it for you." That promise made Veronica smile. "And never forget, my sweet sister. God is for us. And mother, wherever she may be. He will never forsake us or the family."

The two sisters disappeared into the house garden to a crescendo of singing birds and a light breeze whistling through the trees.

The two months that Veronica waited for Marcos' arrival felt more like two years. Her patience had run dry and her eagerness to see him had grown as high as an old oak tree.

On his arrival, he stayed in a cheap, rundown hotel just a short bus ride away. His first meeting with the family was both respectful and comfortable, sitting in the garden around the white painted table, enjoying ice-cold drinks beneath the hazy sun. Marcos spoke confidently of his life and family back home in Itaim and of his profession. He felt that a positive connection had been made when it was agreed that he could spend tomorrow with Veronica sightseeing in Rio.

They spent a week together in Rio, enjoying each other's company. With every passing day, she discovered something new that she liked about him and she felt that there was something strong growing between them. Even after his return home, they would spend endless hours talking on the phone and sending letters and postcards to each other. It was a difficult way to run a relationship, being so far apart but it just seemed so right. The sound of the ringing phone was Veronica's highlight of the day, drawn to it like a dog to its master.

After eight months of unorthodox dating, Marcos asked her if she'd perhaps like to get engaged. Her graduation was also fast approaching and was already acting as an intern at the school. Without hesitation, she accepted his offer.

The news was welcomed not just by her family but also friends from all around Rio. Her bridal outfits were ready after a couple of months, designed and conceived from gifts donated by those close to the family. But Veronica still felt uneasy and stressed about her secretive past. The skeleton that she hid in her closet regularly came calling like a thundercloud on a family picnic. She once again sought advice from Flora about how this was making her feel and, her level-headed, sensible sister suggested that maybe it was time to tell him all about it. She could not start a new life and marriage with this hanging over her head and the truth had to be told before a wedding date was set.

It took just three days for Marcos to arrive in Rio after Veronica's invitation during one of their endless telephone calls. Although she desperately wanted to see him, she also dreaded his arrival. Their pending conversation terrified her and filled her entire soul with apprehension.

She feared that he would somehow blame her and walk out of her life forever. All her life, she had been the ultimate pessimist and found it very difficult to stream positive thoughts and emotions. Marcos was the best thing that had ever happened to her and had converted her tormented life into something fresh and exciting. He gave her a reason to get out of bed in the morning, to face the challenges presented to her each day. She felt happy, loved and cherished.

Veronica invited him to go for ice cream at the popular parlour adjacent to the local post office. She wanted to avoid the prying eyes and listening ears of the family, thus allowing her to do it her way. Marcos sensed that something was troubling his fiancée and was happy to follow her lead, like a little lost puppy. He did not press or pressure her but waited for her to reveal all in her own time. She appreciated his sensitivity and consideration.

They sat down on a vacant bench outside the parlour, ice creams in hand. Veronica licked a splash of cream from her finger and looked Marcos directly in the eyes. She held a serious frown on her face, an unhappy frown. "Before we set a date for our wedding, I need to tell you something," she said. "It's something that happened to me a long time ago and I feel you need to know. I can't start a new life with you with this hovering over me."

"You look so serious, sweetheart. What's wrong?"

As she told him the story, she found herself remarkably calm and in control of her emotions. Marcos listened and hung on to every word she said without interruption. His facial expressions changed as the details became more graphic.

Occasionally she would pause for a moment to allow passers-by to move out of earshot.

Marcus sat in silence for a moment, digesting her words. He rose sharply from his seat, dropping the ice cream on the pavement. His anger was frightening, his face turning red in a fit of rage. "I'm going to kill him." No other words came from his lips.

"Sit down, Marcos, please," Veronica begged him. "Please sit and calm down," she continued, gesturing her hand toward the bench. Marcus stood motionless for a few moments before slumping back into his seat. "Think about what you are saying, for god's sake. If he dies, my virtue goes with him and you go to prison. We will forever be unhappy like him. To me, he is very unhappy, and it makes me feel good to know that each and every day, he kills himself a little more."

Veronica fell silent, waiting for a response that never came. "So now you know," she said. "I hope this doesn't change your feelings for me." Still, no response came in the moment of silence as Marcos looked down at his shoes. Veronica took a deep breath. "Do you still want to get married?"

Marcus looked up immediately and smiled. "Of course I do," he promised. "These changes nothing. Marrying you will show this pig that the world is not just full of evil people." He put his hand on hers. "And don't think I am marrying you just to make amends for what he did to you, nor out of pity. I am marrying you because I love you." His words were genuine and full of sincerity. Veronica smiled.

They both agreed that the wedding would take place in four months, leaving them plenty of time to arrange the dress, organise and dispatch the many invitations, book the ceremonies and prepare the buffet for over one hundred guests. There would be two ceremonies for their special union, not legally required but a popular choice for many marrying couples in Brazil; the legal wedding, in a registry office, was booked and planned for a Wednesday morning and the religious ceremony was booked for the following Saturday at the quaint local church perched up on the hill.

Wednesday's event, attended by family members, was a wonderful, happy day that went well with no problems. So much laughter with everyone in high spirits and one or two family guests drinking just a little too much! It was a beautiful beginning for Marcos and Veronica to start their lives together.

But sadly, it didn't last. On Friday morning, Marcos received a call from his father informing him that his mother back in Sao Paulo had fallen ill, just as his family was due to depart for Rio. His mother and father insisted that Saturday's church ceremony be postponed for a later date as Marcus was their only son and they were desperate to see him become a groom. Neither bride nor groom were happy with a cancellation but Marcos knew that it had to be. Veronica took it hard and was clearly upset about it, ensuring that Marcos knew how she felt.

"You're crazy, Marcos," she implied. "There are one hundred plus guests coming from all over the country. Our wedding is tomorrow. We've contracted and paid for the catering service and you want to postpone. It's not going to happen. We are not going to disappoint all of our guests. Think of all the shame that will befall my family." She shook her head in defiance. "I won't let it happen."

Marcos stepped forward and took her into his arms, cuddling his new wife tightly. "I understand all of that," he whispered softly in her ear. "But how could I forgive myself if, god forbid, my mother died? I could never cope with that." He released her from his grip and kissed her gently on the cheek. "There is no argument here," he continued. "We must cancel. At least for now. We are already husband and wife so it's no big deal to reschedule the church. We can do that at a more appropriate time."

After requesting permission and being granted by Veronica, he approached Zilar and her husband to apologise for the chaos and trouble caused and that he needed to return home post haste. He also insisted that, as they were married now, Veronica went with him and that they would return at a later date to collect her belongings. Without hesitation, they both unconditionally agreed.

Zilar wandered over to Veronica, who was standing alone by the unfilled buffet tent, observing the events unfolding before her eyes. "Don't worry about the arriving guests," she explained. "Nor the caterers or the church. We'll sort it out somehow, I promise you. Your place is now by your husband's side."

She looked round at Marcos, who stood alone in the garden like a guy on a street corner. "Marcus tells me that your apartment is ready for you to occupy. That is so very important. The time has come for you to leave here and start your new with life your husband. It would be nice if everything always went to plan but unfortunately is doesn't. There is nothing we can do about this. Bide your time and the church ceremony will happen for you one day."

Zilar lovingly hugged her little sister and wished her good luck and, in just a few moments, she was gone.

In less than two hours, husband and wife were sitting in the airport departure lounge, waiting to board a flight to Sao Paulo. Very few words were exchanged. What was supposed to be the happiest time of both their lives had turned into an unwanted melodrama. Words were not needed right now, just a showing of collective love and affection with the occasional cuddle and the touching of hands was enough. Their emotion of complete sadness had hit them like a freight train at high speed. It wasn't supposed to happen like this.

The flight was short and they soon arrived at their new home, where they duly dumped the single bag and immediately headed for the hospital. Marcos' mother lay in a bed in the far corner of the ward. They walked along the aisle between the two rows of beds, a squeak occasionally sounding from the sole of Marcus' shoes from the well-polished, shiny floor. Upon seeing them, his mother did not speak but expressed an air of joy at their arrival.

Sitting in the provided chairs around the bed were his father and two sisters. After greeting each other with a kiss or touch of a hand, his father offered his apologies for what had happened. A helpful nurse bought two more chairs for the new arrivals and they all settled around the bed. The newly-weds stayed all night so that the others could take an uncomfortable nap in the far from comfortable chairs. For a number of weeks, doctors and nurses came and went, as did the visitors and eventually, Marcos' mother was discharged to return home.

Marcos and Veronica began to settle into their new lives together but she still felt an element of frustration as she still dreamed of having the religious ceremony at the church. Her frustration was obvious to some but not to others, but she continued to hold restraint on how she felt. She said nothing of this to her husband, as she didn't want to upset the applecart or cause any friction. As her father once told her many years ago, 'you are to be seen and not heard!'

Despite still being just eighteen years old, she showed remarkable dedication to her marriage and worked tirelessly to build a strong and united family. Her days saw the apartment well cared for, clean, tidy and organised and her nights saw her as passionate and willing to please her husband sexually. She had her part-time job but still found time to complete the household chores.

Over the next eight years, they endured many ups and downs. She mothered five children; four girls and a boy, each one a bright light in her life. On the other side of the coin, Marcos became a drug addict; snorting cocaine and regularly smoking hash cannabis. He tried a number of times to get clean but always relapsed and slipped into his old ways. His habit put tremendous pressure on the household finances, as well as inflicting much pain and suffering in the family home.

Two of the children, Ana Beatriz and Luciana, were now in elementary school and little Isabella was attending kindergarten. Veronica employed a helper to ease the workload she had to endure. Elena would take the girls to school every day as part of her many duties, which proved to be a great help. It allowed Veronica to start a second job, which was very much needed but kept her away from home all day, every day, including weekends.

For a long time now, Marcos had led an upside-down life, sleeping all day and staying up throughout the night. He struggled to keep a job for any length of time and was becoming more and more impatient with the two youngest children, Junior and Anna Luiza.

As a result, Veronica was forced to take on the responsibility of supporting the family all alone. But as always, she stood her ground. On the occasional Sunday, they would all go to Marcos' parents' home for lunch. His whole family knew that he was on the drugs again. Veronica told her mother-in-law that the situation had reached breaking point and was close to the point of no return.

It was getting far too difficult for her to support everything by herself and was struggling to cope. He stayed out all night, nearly every night, doing god knows what with god knows who, returning home just as she was leaving for work. Not a single kiss or cuddle. Not even a simple hello. Nothing but a look of disrespect. It was as if he didn't know who she was anymore.

Her mother-in-law held a blank look on her face as she listened to Veronica's words. She knew exactly what was going on. "You know, I have given all of my money to him for expenses or whatever he needs it for," she told her. "I have nothing left in the bank, it's all gone, every last penny. All I can offer you right now is my food leftovers once a week, after I clean out the fridge. There is usually quite a lot of waste I throw away but you can have it. It's not going to be fresh but it is OK to eat."

She seemed embarrassed at making such an offer. "I told him this already but he didn't care. My words just go in one ear, then out of the other."

"I don't think that you realise what's really happening here," Veronica guessed. "None of the money you have given him was spent on our home or the children. And certainly not on me. He uses it to buy the drugs he needs. Do you think that with my two jobs and with me cooking cheap meals every evening, that he would even need to ask you for money. He has been like this for three years. He could be breaking the law in an effort to get his fix. I have no idea."

Veronica halted her words as she tried to assess her next statement. "I think we need to take action. Do something. Get him in a rehab clinic. I don't want to raise my children alone because their father is either in prison or even dead from an overdose. But, if necessary, I will. I have already prepared myself for that scenario. I have been left with no choice."

A cold, eerie silence fell upon them.

Sundays weren't just spent having lunch with the in-laws. In the morning, before the visits, Veronica would take the children to church for morning mass. Since the wedding, she had become quite close to the priest, often visiting him out of hours for a cup of tea and a chat. It had become part of her regular routine and enjoyed the odd afternoon with him when she had the time.

They would talk about everything and nothing most of the time but her nerves were at breaking point and she was desperate to confide in someone. Someone who was impartial. Someone that wouldn't judge or criticise her. Someone that could help and guide her in the right direction.

It was a very difficult conversation for her, exposing the intimate details of her troubled private life. But despite the nature of the chat, she felt relaxed and in total control. The priest had a calming demeanour about him with an attractive smile and a soft, gentle voice. He listened respectfully, offering words of encouragement only when she had paused.

The priest suggested that she try to persuade Marcos to participate in a parish course known as 'Couples Encounter with Christ'. It was an encounter group meeting for troubled couples that were having marriage difficulties. Since its formation two years ago, it had proved to be successful and very helpful for many people.

To her surprise, Marcos agreed to go so Veronica enrolled them both in the ten-week course. There were two sessions each week, each one being two hours long. They indulged in counselling with a professional, had group meetings with other troubled couples and were urged to have one-on-one chats with each other, under supervision. The course was very revealing and a real eye opener for them both. Veronica was stunned at how much she know about her husband and how much she didn't know.

They saw the course through to the end despite Marcos' objections on occasions, as he 'preferred to do other things'. On its completion, each couple were offered the opportunity to re-take their marriage vowels and those that did were given a free, all expenses paid weekend away trip to Campos do Jordao to restart their lives together.

On this trip, Veronica became pregnant again while her husband, less than a week after the course finished, relapsed and began his drug taking again. Only this time it was with greater impact, not just because he was an addict but also because his friends gave him drugs, even when he had no money to buy them.

The devil had taken him from church attendee to nighttime hooligan, where he began using the family car to go on illegal drag races at dawn in exchange for drugs. His ever-suffering wife, now six weeks pregnant, obtained a severe kidney infection and was ultimately hospitalised for two weeks. She lost her part-time job at the beauty parlour, now leaving her with just the public servant's position. Her point of no return had long passed as she lay in her hospital bed, heavily depressed and full of anxiety.

A tear dripped from her eye, coming to rest on her pillow. Then another and another, like a convoy of buses on the high street. She could not allow another child to be born into this relationship. It was a decision that made her ache with pain but it would only do more harm than good. She could not bring another child into this world only for it so suffer so much as she had. But she would remain silent about it, filing it on the top shelf in her vault of hidden secrets.

She now knew what she had to do. It was as clear as the sky on a beautiful summer's day. Her husband was a weakling, an irresponsible, careless good-for-nothing. He had heavily scarred her for the rest of her life, a hideous injury that would never heal. She took the difficult decision never to have children again, neither with her husband nor from any other man. The thought soaked her pillow even more.

Veronica eventually returned home without a single visit from Marcos. He was either sleeping or breaking the law in some illegal nocturnal venture. Her father-in-law arranged for her discharge from the hospital. Apparently, Marcos was away on some camping trip with his drug induced pals, leaving his lovely *wife*, pregnant and sick, to look after the children.

During his two week camping vacation away from the rigueur of married life, Marcos was arrested during one of his many street races at 2 o'clock in the early morning. In the car, the police discovered a stash of cocaine together with a hand-gun and three bullet magazines. He was arrested and returned to Sao Paulo where he was held in a detention centre. The police also discovered that he was involved in a sexual relationship with an underage girl, the daughter of a friend of his uncle, who was an army commander. Yet another young, innocent girl's life, fallen victim to the evil drug cartels.

After much soul searching and a lot of courage, it was still a difficult choice to visit Marcos at the detention centre. The humiliation was the ultimate embarrassment as she stood in the visitors' queue. On the walls hung information signs such as *You are one step away from hell* and *Do not bring gifts. None of them will be allowed to pass.* And these were the pleasant ones.

On her way through visitors' search, she was forced to strip naked, including her underwear, to be thoroughly checked for drugs, weapons and other contraband. She had to lift both breasts for secreted items and forced to spread her legs as her vagina was inspected by a doctor (or what she hoped was a doctor). The violation was sickening to the core.

With the all clear intact and the guards happy that she wasn't smuggling, she was allowed to dress. They may not have found any banned items but they seem to get a great deal of pleasure from rummaging through the small birthday cake she had bought for him. It finished up as just a pile of destroyed sponge and icing. Read the signs they told her, even though she had. No gifts of any kind.

Veronica nearly broke down at the shocking vision of her husband as he appeared in the visitors' hall. He approached her table slowly with a slight limp and had injuries on his face. He was unrecognisable in his appearance. His hair was falling out and looked heavily malnourished. His detention uniform, yellow with a black strip down the middle, was far too baggy. He had lost so much weight.

Predictably, there were only two items on his agenda for her; the first begging for her forgiveness and second, to get him out of that awful place; making her promise that she would do it. Even though he had built a ton of hardship upon her shoulders and had hurt the children constantly, she could not let him suffer and rot away in that devil's den. He was still her husband and she loved him, even though she was advised.

She left in an awful hurry, desperate to get away from that evil stench of pain and suffering. She was deeply distraught, encased in a world of confusion. After returning home and with Elena minding the children, she contacted a lawyer, recommended by a friendly couple from the church encounter group. He was a distant relation of theirs and managed to negotiate and reduction on his fees. A smartly dressed, well-groomed man with the manners to match. Veronica paid the fee and he began his work.

As the lawyer and his associates worked to free Marcos, Veronica paid a visit to her doctor's surgery who, within days, had arranged a termination at the hospital. Less than three months later, with the help of a bribe or two, Marcos was a free man and Veronica no longer carried a child in her womb.

Immediately after Marcos' release, Veronica began to make all the necessary arrangements to leave her husband. She escorted Ana Beatriz and Luciana to Ines' house in Vitoria, where they would stay for a while.

Ines offered her assistance in any way she could, including help on organising a work transfer for Veronica back home to Vitoria. Happy that the two children were cared for and looked after, she returned to Sao Paulo to visit her mother-in-law. She politely asked if she would look after Anna Luiza, Isabela and Junior for a month or two, until she found a house in Vitoria for her and the children. Mother-in-law implored with her not leave her son, not to separate the children from their father and to take serious time to think about exactly what she was doing.

Veronica adamantly said, "The children and I have suffered enough and I refuse to allow the kids to remain in such a volatile atmosphere. It's highly explosive and he can't be trusted. I will not allow it."

Marcos' father agreed with the very word she said. "They can stay here for as long as you need." His support was very welcoming. "Leave it with us. You must do what you have to do."

She thanked them for their understanding and headed off to the bank, on the corner of Ruiza Avenue and the high street. She was greeted by an elegantly dressed lady with long black hair a stylish pearl necklace proudly hanging from her neck.

Veronica presented the teller with a cheque, withdrawing what little money there was left.

"I'm sorry, ma'am," the teller said. "There is not enough money in your account to make this withdrawal."

"You're kidding me, right?" Her surprise was clearly evident. "There should be more than I am asking for."

"I'm afraid not, ma'am," the teller reaffirms. "A significant withdrawal was made first thing this morning," she explained. "By your husband."

Veronica cursed quietly under her breath and shook her head. "Will this never end?" she mumbled to herself.

"Pardon me, ma'am."

"So when did he—" her words faded into nothing as did the sentence. "Alright, so how much is left in the account?"

The teller wrote the remaining total on the back of a deposit slip and slid it to her under the large glass protective screen.

Again, Veronica cursed beneath her breath as she saw the amount. She carefully tore a second cheque from its book and filled it out with the revised amount, signing the bottom before passing it to the teller. It was barely enough to buy the bus ticket home. After being paid, she placed the money in her purse and stormed through the door.

After returning home, she prepared the three children for their temporary living quarters. Marcos was still not to be seen—Anywhere. She phoned her father-in-law when the children were ready to come and collect them and also happen to mention that he had forged her signature to steal money from her account.

It was becoming a very difficult time for Veronica. Although she was adamant and positive about what she believed in, it sent a cold shiver down her spine. With so many worries and problems standing taller than a grand old oak tree, she would now have to endure the pain of being separated from the children. She just wanted it to all go away but it seemed to just get worse.

With the children now with their grandparents, Veronica prepared for her departure from the bus station. She struggled with two bags: a large luggage bag and a smaller suitcase. Before leaving, she left a quick note for Marcos telling him that the house no longer had an electricity or power. *What a shame*, she thought. He probably won't stay for very long.

The bus station was busy as usual, with lines of buses transporting passengers to the far corners of the country. An idling bus parked at the entrance, its engine running, pumping black, poisonous gases into the enclosed yard. The smell was nauseating and overpowering, causing her to cough. She had arrived without a ticket, being in such a hurry to leave and there were no tickets available for Vitoria for another seven hours; the ten-p.m. departure.

Fortunately for her, however, a young couple were selling theirs for the bus leaving in an hour. She offered to buy one but there were two tickets to sell. After a quick discussion and a large compromise, they agreed to sell her just the one.

Veronica hated the bus journey. She had made the same trip countless time and the buses were uncomfortable, noisy and dirty. Empty drinks cans and bottles rolled aimlessly along the floor, cigarette ends lay motionless in the very corner and dog-eared newspapers and magazines littered the seats. She picked up a partially read monthly and laid it on her lap. It would help pass the time.

She was awoken by the shaking of her shoulders and a muffled voice. "Wake up, lady," it snorted.

Veronica opened her eyes and was greeted by the vision of the bus driver, cigar in mouth, with his cap sitting to one side of his head. His white uniform shirt had the top three buttons undone as the air-conditioning wasn't working. "Hey, lady," he persisted. "It's your stop. Disembark for Vitoria."

Veronica slowly rose to her feet, the monthly magazine falling to the floor to join its other discarded companions. She picked up her two bags that had been made available to her by the driver. Upon leaving the bus, she scanned the scene around her. There was nobody there to meet her. The bus doors closed with a hiss of air and speed away in a cloud of thick black smoke.

For a moment, she stood alone on the street with just her luggage for company. A taxi pulled up before her and the driver leant out of the window. "Taxi, missus?" he offered.

The rugged voice interrupted Veronica's private thoughts. "Yes, yes please," she said. "Could you help me with my bags?"

"What do you think I am, lady? An airport conveyor belt?" His sarcasm was both unwanted and unappreciated. Veronica said nothing, not because it was her way but because this time, she was stunned by his rudeness. The driver sighed in disapproval and sharply opened his cab door. "I guess I was right the first time."

He haphazardly dumped the bags in the boot of his taxi, slammed the door loudly and climbed on to the front seat. Veronica followed suit and they were on their way to her very much awaited destination.

Dusk was calling when she finally knocked on the door. The sweet smell of dinner cooking wafted through an open window. It took a moment for the door to open and there stood her two daughters. Seeing them gave her a feeling that she was actually in a state of grace! "Hello, girls," she greeted. "Have you got a kiss for mum?"

They both tightly hugged her before Ines' maid appeared. "Hello, miss Veronica. Nice to see you," she said. "Ines isn't here just now but allow me to bring in you bags and help you settle in." She was always very polite and accommodating.

Together, they sat down on the spacious sofa while the maid took her bags to one of the bedrooms. The television was on at a low volume, showing children's cartoons. Luciana enquired about her brother and sisters that had remained behind in Sao Paulo with their grandparents.

"Come on, girls," she said. "Come sit here." Veronica tapped the sofa, either side of her with both hands. The girls excitedly got up and danced their way to their mum, each sitting beside her. She placed her arms around them.

"They are all fine," she continued. "All three of them. They are only staying at grandma's for a while. It's not forever. Tomorrow I will start to search for another home for us all and when that happens, they will come and live with us." Veronica smiled at them sweetly, a gesture of reassurance. "All the family back together, as it should be."

Luciana bounced her bottom up and down on the sofa in excitement. "And what about daddy, mum?" she enquired. "When is he coming?"

"Well, daddy will—" Veronica didn't complete her sentence. "Tell you what," she said, quickly changing the subject. "Turn the television off and let's go play in the garden before dinner."

"Yayyyy," came the happy response. The two girls jumped from the sofa and rushed towards the back door. Veronica remained seated for a few moments, before switching the television off and dropping the remote on to the coffee table.

The girls were still playing when Ines strolled confidently through the gate at around 8 o'clock. She saw her sister sitting on the porch in the swing seat, drink in hand. Ines held her arms aloft and called to her. "Nica," she said loudly.

Veronica offered her a wave but remained seated. The two girls also sent her a wave before returning to their fun and games. Ines climbed the six wooden steps leading on to the porch and leant lazily on the seat frame. She took the cold drink from her sister's hand and took a long swig before returning it.

"It's wonderful to have you back, Nica," she said. "We have all been so worried about you. I can't believe how that pig has treated you. You are better to be away from him."

Ines continued by labelling and insulting him with every negative adjective she could muster, showing no respect as to how Veronica was feeling. She ignored her all out assault on her husband as she gently swayed the swing with her feet. After she had finished her insult attack, she placed the plastic bag she was carrying on the wooden floor and sat next to her sister. Joyous, happy voices still sounded playfully from close to the garden fence.

"The girls are so happy that they are where they belong," Ines observed. "It's so lovely to see. I hope you are too."

Veronica gave her a short nod of her head. Her feelings were mixed and full of total confusion. Yes, she was very happy to be home, in the place that she loved and had missed so much while she was away. But the truth of the matter was that she was back for all the wrong reasons. The choices that she had made were forced upon her and all of those difficult decisions would eventually yield consequences, particularly the effects it would have on the children.

She knew that they had to be told sooner or later that their daddy was gone and that they would have to live in a broken family. But how much could she tell them? She did not want to burden the children with tales of drug taking, stealing from the family and breaking the law to get his next fix. She did not want the children to think that this was normal everyday life and that carrying a loaded gun was OK.

The coming weeks were going to be highly challenging and she knew that there were a lot of tears to come. She had already told her sister and other family members not to say anything. That was Veronica's painful duty and, as their mother, she had to accept some of the responsibility for the sake of the children. She didn't feel that any of it was her fault but at the same time, she didn't want the kids growing up, hating their father.

Veronica drained the last of her drink and placed the empty glass on the floor next to the plastic bag. She lifted her feet from the floor so that the seat would swing at its own gentle pace. She looked at Ines, who was watching the girls running in the garden with so much youthful energy. "Have you spoken yet to the Department of Education about my job transfer request?" she asked.

"How long for dinner, mum?" a voice called from the distance.

Veronica did not answer, as there was business to discuss. Ines wasn't sure who had called out but guessed it was Luciana, as they were hidden by the large holly bush in the centre of the garden. "Yes, I meant to tell you, "She told Veronica. "You have an interview scheduled for two days' time. That'll be Friday. It's at the local office in town. There's a confirmation letter inside that you have to take with you."

"OK, thank you." She placed her feet flat on the floor, halting the swing in its tracks.

"Nica, you understand that you need to pass this interview," Ines warned her. "If you fail for any reason, you won't get the transfer."

"Yes, I realise that but it's not for a new job. It's just for a transfer so it should be alright."

"I hope you won't be so complacent on Friday. This is important."

Veronica rose from the seat in preparation to go inside. "Do you know what the working hours are for this position?"

Ines copied her sister and jumped to her feet. "It's the morning shift, eight until one." She took a step forward and leant on her forearms on the verandas' guard rail. "Come on, girls," she instructed. "Time to clean up before dinner." She heard moans of disapproval but still couldn't see them in the vast garden space.

They all made their way inside the house and Veronica slowly and gently closed the door behind them.

Veronica was up and awake by the crack of dawn. Through the window, the sun had barely made its presence felt as it began to rise above the distant hills, yet the birds were already singing joyfully as they celebrated a new morning. A dull murmur of passing traffic could be heard, like a talentless, tone-deaf musical band. It was already excessively warm after a humid night. She switched on the ceiling fans in the living room and then the kitchen, allowing the fresh air to circulate and cool down the house before other signs of life appeared from their rooms.

Soon the house would be full of screaming kids, complaining sisters and vacuum cleaners commanded by the maids. Not that she was unappreciative of Ines' help. She had broken the chain of the heartbreak hotel in Sao Paulo, even though the links were weak with rust for a long time and now her destiny was in her own hands. She had had to be strong and tough through much of her tormented life and her marriage failure was just an extension of that. Again and again she had proven herself in times of adversity but with time and god as friendly allies, she knew that one day she'd be able to proudly hold her head high once more.

There was so much to do and prepare for. Her interview tomorrow was top of the priority list. The job transfer would be a titanic step forward to recovery and would go a long way towards having her own home again.

After breakfast, she planned to go to town in search of a second job, working in a beauty salon. She had all the necessary qualifications and experience and once running her own small business, would surely hold her in good stead. A second job would be a true godsend and speed up her house application. At the moment, it was all conjecture and definitely premature but the omens were positive. It gave her a warm feeling inside.

She left the house before anyone else was awake. Ines had the morning off work and wasn't expected in until midday. As for the children; they had run themselves in to the ground with their exertions in the garden. Veronica expected them to sleep in until at least lunch time.

It took her about twenty minutes to walk in to town, arriving at 9 o'clock, just as the shops and business were starting their busy days. Veronica recalled there being three salons along the high street but that number could have changed over her long absence. It was already busy as she strolled along the vast avenue.

Shop keepers were moving their merchandise on to the pavement in preparation for a sale. Buses, cars and noisy motorbikes populated the busy road like a nest of angry ants in search of food to devour. Passers-by and shoppers scuttled by, occasionally stopping to window shop at some expensive boutique while others popping in to the butchers to purchase fresh meat for tonight's dinner.

As she approached the main junction with Teixa Boulevard, she noticed a new salon on the corner. It was new as she remembered that it used to be a food takeaway restaurant, selling mainly pizzas in its heyday. From across the road, she could clearly see inside the establishment. It was a huge and very elegant building with two large windows on either side of its entrance. The windows revealed it as a busy, bustling place full of clientele being pampered or in waiting. The receptionist was constantly on the phone, taking bookings, Veronica guessed. This was the place that she sought.

Veronica briskly crossed the road as the traffic lights turned red and confidently walked in. It took a few moments for her eyes to adjust from the brightness outside to the sparsely lit interior of the shop. An air-conditioner hummed persistently as she slowly approached the receptionist, looking around as she did, getting a feel of the place.

"Hello," the receptionist pleasantly greeted, after replacing the phone back on its receiver. "I'm Carman. How can I help you?"

Before Veronica could reply, the phone rang again but was ignored. "Hi. I was wondering if I could speak with the manager," Veronica asked, carefully laying a clear plastic folder on the desk.

"Off course." She stood up and gestured to a man that was pinning fliers on to the notice board.

The man walked over, putting a few multi-coloured pins in his pocket. He was a tall, overweight man with dark hair that was thinning on top. He wore a cheap blue pinstripe summer suit with three pens perched in its breast pocket.

Veronica met him halfway across the floor and offered her hand as a greeting. He shook it. "What can I do for you, miss?"

"Actually, I was looking for work," Veronica explained. "I have just moved back here from Sao Paulo and I'm available to start immediately."

"I see. Come to my office."

On their way past, Veronica collected her folder from the reception desk. She was led in to a surprisingly small office, not much bigger than a box room in a small house. The desk occupied most of its space with two filing cabinets behind it, forcing him to turn his chair sideways in order to allow him to sit down.

"What's your name?" he asked.

"Errr, Veronica," she smiled. She was expecting him to reveal his but didn't.

"Please sit," he said, as he took a cigarette from a draw. He tapped it on the desk a few times before lighting it. "OK, so you are after some work, then." He tipped his head backwards in order to blow the smoke upwards. "What can you offer me?"

Veronica opened the folder and removed a small pile of papers, laying them tidily on a disorganised, messy desk. "I have qualifications in facial aesthetics," she said. "I took and passed a course in Sao Paulo a few months ago." She handed the papers to the manager. "These are my certificates and professional references. Everything is there, everything you need. Please feel free to contact whoever you need to."

The manager set his cigarette in the half filled ashtray as he casually flicked through the paperwork, offering the odd facial expression. "There isn't much call for this here," he said, returning the papers to her. "Our forte here is mainly hairdressing, manicure, pedicure and body waxing," he continued. "Customers go elsewhere if they want a beauty facial."

She neatly collected the papers and tucked them back in to the folder. "There is a lot I can offer you. Pedicure, hairdressing, facial. They are all part of the same beauty business. Your profits would only go up with this inclusion."

He took a long drag of his cigarette as he processed her statement. She had a point. "I tell you what," he said as the smoke cascaded from his mouth. "I'll see what I can do for you. I'll promote your business to the customers and advertise it in the salon. If it yields any business, I'll call you with the details. But understand, I'm not promising you anything right now. Let's see how it pans out." He paused before continuing, "If this brings you work, then forty percent of the profits go to the salon and you get the rest."

Veronica wasn't a natural businesswoman so couldn't be sure if those numbers were a fair deal or not, but it was an income. She nodded her head in agreement, collected her folder and left the cool salon interior for the increasing heat outside.

The following day, Veronica attended her long awaited interview at the Secretary of Education. It had been a nervous time for her as it approached because there was so much was hinging on its outcome. She had prepared fully, dressed appropriately and prayed continuously and she now felt she could take on the world.

Her confidence was fully justified. The interview went so well, it felt like it was a foregone conclusion; as if the contract had been stamped weeks before. The letter of confirmation dropped through the letter box just days later, together with an already booked an appointment with the school's headmaster. That meeting saw them fine tune the final details and a start date at the school was agreed.

Veronica felt on top of the world. Her long suffering life was now falling nicely in to place and for the first time in a long time, the seas were blue and the skies were clear. Soon a regular wage would be coming in together with her boutique salary. It wasn't really a boutique, just a salon but when happiness takes a hold of you so strongly, you are entitled to exaggerate. Soon it would be time for her to search for a new home and the family would all be together again. With so much good news, it was easy to forget what she had left behind, drifting further away in her tunnel of life.

It wasn't an easy routine to master. In fact, it bought many problems and hardships but with her perseverance and organisation skills, Veronica easily managed to multi-task her two jobs and, at the same time, care for the girls. She was leading a hectic lifestyle and yet, Ana Beatriz and Luciana had everything they could ask for.

Her freelancing at the beauty parlour had become an instant hit with the customers, with her appointment ledger becoming full. Already, she had to decline two new customers of appointments, rescheduling them to suit her time rather than theirs. And with all that going on, she still managed to find time to shop around for a new home.

She had viewed three or four possible choices but they were unacceptable for many different reasons. Veronica had moved from pillar to post all her life and she wanted, once and for all, to settle down in the home of her choosing and stay there. Her final choice had to be the right one, not just for her but also all the children and, looking through the window of an estate agent adjacent to her workplace, she saw exactly what she was looking for.

Drawn to it like a bee to a flower, she went straight inside and within fifteen minutes, had secured a viewing, despite the property agent trying to interest her in something bigger and much more expensive.

The house sat on the summit of a steep hill and commanded beautiful views of the surrounding area and the low mountain range in the far distance. A fast-flowing stream ran past at the bottom of the garden and in the evening, when the traffic had died down, she could hear the cool fresh water as it cascaded and caressed the rocks. The garden wasn't enormous but was sizeable, giving the children somewhere to play safely. It had three bedrooms so one would be a little full but the kids would love to share a room together.

The neighbourhood was classed as crime free by the Office of National Statistics but not completely. No village, town or city was totally immune. Veronica decided this was the home she wanted even before she had walked through the front door and the icing on the cake; Ines was just a half hour's walk away.

With the deposit and one month's rent in advance paid and, with the help of those around her, they moved in. It was partially furnished before she obtained the keys and the rest of the furniture would be delivered in stages from shops and local business. The time had finally come to bring the three children from Sao Paulo home.

Veronica phoned her mother-in-law, asking her to meet her at the bus station with the children. Instead of pain and sadness, happiness was dominating her life now and she did not want to see, hear or speak to her husband. If anyone could ruin a beautiful moment, he was him and she wanted no part of it. She took the overnight bus, only managing to sleep in stages. But she didn't care, it was all part of the grand plan to restart her life and see the children growing up happy and content, absent from such a volatile atmosphere.

As the bus pulled in to the bustling station, Veronica could see them standing on the cat-walk, each holding a bag of sweets. She tapped heavily on the window with her knuckles and sent them a wave and a smile when they saw her happy face. She rushed off the bus after it had parked up and raced over to them.

Conflicting emotions dominated her body, pulling her in a thousand different directions, great sadness joined with utter joy. They all joined together in an emotional family hug, locking arms around waists and hands stroking faces. Muffled voices sounded illegible from the tight squeeze. One of them had burst in to tears or was it all of them? It didn't matter one bit as their long, ten-week ordeal had come to an end.

Amongst the carnage unfolding on the cat-walk of the bus station, mother and father-in-law stood together, hand in hand, watching.

Chapter Five

The in-laws again continued to apologise to Veronica for their sons' inexcusable and unacceptable behaviour and the way he had treated his family. She was desperate to catch the next bus home to Vitoria and as they talked on, Veronica found it difficult to interact. She constantly scanned the area, hoping and praying that Marcos didn't suddenly and miraculously appear from some dark, secluded alleyway.

The bus was overdue, already running five minutes late and her impatience and nervousness was increasing. Junior was holding her hand, as if he could sense her trepidation. Anna Luizan and Isabela were both saying their goodbyes, sweets in hand.

The bus appeared, held up briefly by a red traffic light before slowly easing its way into a reserved parking space. A dozen or so passengers exited before Veronica hurriedly ushered the children in. She quickly hugged her in-laws and thanked them for all their assistance and help.

In return, they wished her well and good luck for the future. After climbing the three steps on to the bus, the automatic doors closed with a squeak and a hiss and the engine revved noisily as it inched towards the main road. Moments later, the bus disappeared from view, carrying Veronica and the children on their journey to freedom.

The kids behaved impeccably throughout the whole journey. Normally, they would be running up and down the aisle, screaming loudly as they played, to the annoyance and frustration of their fellow passengers. Today, though, they were calm and pacified. Well behaved. Perhaps they had had a busy morning, burning excessive energy in the garden before they left. *It was lovely to see*, Veronica thought. Almost serene.

Junior sat quietly next to mum, his head resting on the bus window, watching the world go by, his eyes briefly following objects that caught his interest before moving on to the next one. Isabella and Anna Luizan sat quietly behind them, the occasional rustling sound of paper could be heard as they chomped on their treats. She suspected that they were curious about their dad and wondered why he wasn't travelling with them. The questions would come eventually and Veronica would navigate that route when it came. She hoped that nothing was asked until they arrived home. She did not want to share such a tragic story with strangers.

She was so tired, almost exhausted. Sleeping on these uncomfortable seats would be easy. Her eyelids felt heavy, her legs ached as did her feet. Concentration was lacking severely and she found it a real struggle to do the simplest of tasks. The three days off work she had arranged would be so welcome and once the children were settled in and organised, her much needed rest would follow. The very thought of it made her feel even more tired.

There was so much joy as they arrived at their new home but once again sadness always loitered close by, menacingly. The children revelled in being together as a family once more. As Veronica watched them celebrate their reunion, Ines casually strolled up to her, also watching the enjoyment that was had by them all.

She stood beside her sister, placing a hand on her shoulder. "Have you told them yet?" she inquired. "Do they know?"

Veronica looked at her sister. There was a hint of fear and or trepidation in her eyes. Ines knew her sister inside out and the look she gave her said it all. Veronica shook her head slowly. "What will I tell them? What can I say?" Her words were genuinely full of dread. "I'm trying to build a new life here, for us all and the last thing we need is a spanner in the works. I don't want to upset them and make them cry. I don't really know how they'll all react. Not for sure. They might be OK about it, especially as they are all together again and living in this beautiful new home."

Veronica folded her arms as she watched them dancing in the garden. "I have feared this moment ever since I decided to leave him and now that moment is knocking on the door. I am just terrified I'll hurt them."

Ines removed her hand from her shoulder and stepped directly into her eye line. She placed her index finger under her chin and gently guided her head to her left. "Nica," she said sympathetically. "Look at me. Come on, look at me."

Veronica did as request. "No matter what happens, sister, they have to be told and the sooner the better. You cannot hide it in the closet for ever. The sooner they know, the sooner you and the kids can move on from this. You have already shown your strength and make lots of changes, all for the better and this is the final hurdle for you to negotiate." Ines fell silent as she summoned courage from her soul. "Would you like me to do it?"

"No." Her answer was immediate and decisive. "No, they need to hear it from me, nobody else."

"I have always supported you and helped you in your hour of need and I'm not about to stop now. Just say the word if you change your mind."

Veronica diverted her attention back to the children. "It's fine." She smiled at Ines. "I'll talk to them after dinner. I don't want you to say anything but I'd appreciate it if you sat with me."

"That's the least I can do for my wonderful sister."

Dinner was awkward for the adults as they ate mainly in silence. The children, however, enjoyed their meals in between the sounds of gay laughter and chit chat. Veronica debated whether this was the right time to talk to them, as she was so tired. She just wanted to retire to her bedroom and hibernate for a week but her sister was right, as usual. Holding back was a worthless exercise and counterproductive.

On completion of their meals, they all adjourned to the spacious living room, where the children all sat together on the sofa and Veronica and Ines sat at the coffee table. The maid began to clear the dining table in preparation for washing up.

It was a hard conversation to direct. Veronica spoke slowly and clearly, as she didn't want to have to keep repeating herself. She wanted it over and done with as soon as possible. The children listened for a while without interruption but soon the questions flooded in. Veronica calmly answered them, giving the least amount of detail as she could. Too much of it would be too much for their young minds. Tears began to flow as they digested all that their mum had said.

They may have all been very young but they still fully understood the implications, all except for Junior, who could not hold his attention for very long. It was the eldest, Ana Beatriz, that had shown any maturity. Fast approaching thirteen years old, she had proven herself to be a strong, versatile and an understanding young lady. She was clearly upset but took it upon herself to comfort her siblings; to assure them that it was going to be alright.

They all looked upto her and saw her as their big sister. Her influence was startling as they seemed to calm down a little as the tears stopped. Ana Beatriz's reaction took Veronica by surprise and was mildly shocked at her behaviour.

There had been no signs of her showing compassion before but, nevertheless, was highly appreciative of her thoughtfulness. After the discussion had finished and the children wandered off to do their own things, she took her daughter and gave her a tight cuddle.

Although Ines had remained silent throughout, she had fought back the tears but inside, she was weeping constantly.

With the children happily playing together and Ines staying the night, Veronica ambled slowly to her bedroom, undressed herself and without even brushing her teeth, climbed in to bed. Within seconds, she had fallen in to a deep, undisturbed sleep.

Over the next few days, the children seemed to accept more and more, that their father wasn't coming home. It was Junior and Anna Luiza that found it hardest to cope but Ana Beatriz continued to take the lead role of sympathiser, especially as their mother was now back at work. Both at home and at school, she would always be there for them, like a mother hen caring for her chicks. She did it not because she had to. It was in her nature and was compelled to do it. It wasn't an inconvenience nor a chore; it was the love for her siblings that guided and advised her.

One day, at school, she was called for by a teacher as Junior was having a particularly bad episode and took him from lessons to see the on sight nurse. She sat with him until the headmaster gave permission for them to go home. Their mother had been informed so cancelled her final beauty appointment at the parlour and rushed home as she wanted to be there when the nurse arrived with the children.

She was greeted by the maid, who was in the kitchen ironing a large pile of newly washed clothes. The radio played quietly in the background.

The maid stood the steaming iron upright on its board and greeted her. "Hello, miss Veronica. Welcome home," she said. "Please try not to make too much noise as your husband is sleeping upstairs."

"I beg your pardon."

"Your husband is here. He is asleep in your room."

The words hit her like a steel hammer impacting an anvil. This was not what Veronica wanted to hear. The children were beginning to settle down in their new lives without him and he suddenly turns up unannounced and without warning. His unwelcome presence was not acceptable and would do nothing but disrupt the children's routines.

Veronica began to ascend the stairs when she saw a German shepherd puppy dog standing in the hallway, looking inquisitively at her.

"Where on earth did this dog come from?" she asked the maid.

"Your husband bought it with him." Her replying voice travelled cleanly through the kitchen door. The puppy look round as she spoke, then diverted its attention back to the stranger standing on the stairs.

Veronica looked at the puppy for a moment, its ears erect and eyes alert. She sighed quietly as she climbed the stairs, using the banister for support. The puppy moved to the bottom of the stairs and watched her until she disappeared from view. She hesitantly walked through the open door and saw Marcos lying there in *her* bed. She felt uneasy and uncomfortable as she stood in the doorway.

Marcos stirred and rolled over, as if he was aware of her presence in the room. He hoisted himself up on to his elbows and glared menacingly at her.

"What the hell are you doing here, Marcos?" Her words were direct and to the point. "Who said you could come here?"

"Since when did I need an invitation to see my kids?" He peeled back the duvet and swung his legs from the bed to the floor. He was naked. Veronica averted her eyes and looked away. It shouldn't have come as a surprise, as he never wore anything in bed. "Would you pass me my Flamengo shirt, if you don't mind," he continued, pointing at the chair beside her.

Veronica grabbed the football shirt and threw it harshly at him, landing perfectly on his shoulder. "Where are the kids?" he asked, putting the shirt on in a haphazard, untidy fashion.

"They are where they are supposed to be, at school," she told him. "Something you'd know nothing about." Veronica bundled the rest of his untidily stacked clothes off the chair and on to the floor and sat down. "You can't stay here," she insisted. "Or I should say, you aren't staying here. I want you out of here and take the dog with you. No pets are allowed in this house."

Marcos stood up, allowing his shirt to stretch out. It barely covered his waist. He smiled. "No need to be so coy, my sweet loving wife," he smirked. "There's nothing here that you haven't seen before."

He walked over and picked up his clothes from the floor. "So, who is going to kick me out of this *beautiful* house? You—or your lover?" He stepped back and placed the clothes on the bed. He sat down on its corner and fished out two black coloured socks and preceded to put them on. He looked her directly in the eyes. "I'm sure you have a lover, a slapper like you, living with *my* children."

"You have no idea what you are talking about. Since when did you ever take any interest in me or the children? We were never a priority to you. The only motivation you ever had was preparing for your next score and fix." She stood up and leant against the door frame. "You have no idea what you have done to the children and who has to always pick up the pieces—me." She poked her index finger into her ribs, as if reinforcing her statement. "I want you out," she commanded as she left the bedroom. "And take the dog with you."

The puppy was still at the bottom of the stairs, as if waiting. He was smelling a pair of slippers that sat underneath the shoe stand. When she came in to view, he looked up as she descended the stairs before returning to his nose exploration. She went to the kitchen where the maid was putting on her coat.

"No need for you to get the kids from school," she said. "I'll do it. You just carry on with what you are doing. Ana Beatriz and Junior should be home soon. Junior had a bad day so the nurse is bringing them. When they arrive, give them something to eat and sit them in front of the TV." She halted at the kitchen door and turned around. "I have told Marcus to leave so hopefully he'll be gone when I come back," she explained. "Don't interact with him, OK. And don't do anything for him."

The maid nodded in agreement as she watched Veronica leave. Seconds later, she heard the front door close.

It would normally take about forty minutes to collect the children from school and return home but Veronica deliberately slowed, in order to give more time for Marcos to get out. She took the three children to the ice cream parlour where they sat down while eating. As she waited for them to finish, Veronica watched passers-by as they ambled past, receiving a wave from across the road from one of her neighbours. She felt alienated; it was her own home but didn't want to go there. The very thought sent shivers down her spine but she had to bite the bullet. Maybe he had paid heed and had actually gone.

But no. No such luck. When they arrived home, he was still there, chatting and playing with Junior and Ana Beatriz on the sofa, a can of beer sitting on the coffee table taken from *her* fridge. Upon seeing him, the other three rushed over to him, all trading hugs and kisses. Veronica shook her head in disbelief and walked past them in to the kitchen. It made her feel sick.

Despite how she was feeling, she allowed the children to spend time with their father, even though he had had no previous interest before. She helped the maid with her duties in the kitchen but watched and listened intently to the events unfolding in the living room. She allowed it to continue for a couple of hours before she asked to speak to him in private. They both went to the garden, sitting at the table on the lawn.

Veronica pointed a finger at him and said, "You won't be staying here ever again, is that clear? I asked you to go but you refused so I will arrange to have you removed tomorrow."

He smiled at her, one that combined infuriation and anger. "I didn't break in to this house," he commented. "The door was opened for me."

"The maid let you in because you said that you were my husband. She didn't know what else to do." Veronica shook her head. "I should have prepared her in case of this scenario."

"You are very quick to criticise others but you should take a look in the mirror. You are not so perfect, are you?"

"I don't claim to be. I'm just doing what is best for the kids. Anyway, it's typical of you to take advantage of a situation like this. You should be ashamed of yourself. Why don't you do the right thing for once in your life? Go away and never come back."

"No matter what you do or say, you will not stop me from seeing my kids. It's as simple as that."

Her night was sleepless as she pondered a solution to the situation, dozing fitfully if she was lucky. For long periods of time, she sat up in bed with the lamp on, deep in thought. Downstairs, she could hear the puppy whimpering sometimes, the poor little thing. Marcos was fast asleep on the sofa, tucked up in dreamland while, as usual, she was left to do all the worrying.

The following morning saw the children ready and waiting to go to school when Veronica awoke. She always took the children to school when she had a work shift to attend but today, choosing not to go. Her priority now was to sort out this unwanted problem that was placing her life in limbo. She asked the maid, whose day had long since started, to take them but Marcos quickly stepped in, offering to do it himself. Her answer was an adamant no, no chance, as they had an important matter to resolve. The maid gathered the children, bags and lunch boxes in hand and led them out hurriedly through the front door.

Veronica made her way wearily to the kitchen, filled the kettle and switched it on. Marcos followed on behind her and sat at the large table.

"You still think I am leaving here, do you?" he said. "I don't think so. I've got nowhere to go and I have no money. And I'm not sleeping on the streets with all the other dropouts. I need time to find work and get settled in."

From the cupboard on the wall, she removed one cup, poured in a small amount of milk and added two teaspoons of sugar as she waited for the kettle to boil. She did not look at him. "So you are planning to move here then, are you?" she observed. "Why don't you just stay with your parents in Sao Paulo? You really haven't got the message yet, have you? You are not wanted here."

Marcus watched as she spooned some coffee into her cup. "Try telling that to the kids," he simply said.

"Let me understand. You are moving here to Vitoria where you have no relatives and no money and you just expect me to accommodate you." Veronica picked up the whistling kettle and proceeded to fill her cup. "Take me for granted, why don't you?"

He watched as the rising steam from the kettle evaporated in the air. Veronica put the kettle on the worktop and leant on the tall fridge-freezer.

"Don't do me any favours, will you?" Sarcasm was always one of his traits. He rose his hand and pointed his finger at her. "You are my wife and the mother to my kids," he reminded her.

The words he shouted stabbed into her brain like a thousand simultaneous knives. She slammed her cup down heavily, spilling hot coffee over her hand. "What the hell are you talking about?" she screamed at him with total loss of control. "You have no inclination of the responsibilities I have to endure. None whatsoever. I work fifteen-hour days, holding down two jobs and caring for the children. Scrimping and saving so that the kids have a school uniform to wear and you have the audacity and nerve to call me your wife."

Shouting at him was always ill-advised but sometimes it was the only way to get through to his stubborn head. "You have no idea what is synonymous with your wife, children or family. Why don't you just piss off and disappear forever? Go and tell your *sad* story to someone else because all I expect from you right now is a divorce."

Marcus stood up from the table, creating a grating sound as the chair legs rubbed along the floor. Without a word, but in ferocious anger, he stormed at Veronica and grabbed her by the throat. "I will never give you that," she screamed at her. "You hear me? Never!"

The terror in Veronica's eyes seemed to urge him on. He threw her violently to the polished, tiled floor, sliding uncontrollably until she impacted the hard wood of the table leg. Spots of blood from her wounded head appeared on the white floor like an artist painting a sun setting sky. He began to kick her all over her body, landing each blow with distinct accuracy. like a crescendo of bass drum beats. The dull thuds made a sickening sound with each impact and somewhere above that aggressive baseline, she could hear him scream, 'I'll kill you but I won't divorce you, bitch.'

Veronica somehow managed to scream amidst the terrifying onslaught heard by neighbours that were picnicking in their garden. They rushed to her front door, hammering loudly on the thick, hard wood. "Veronica, are you OK?" the man called. "What's going on?"

"For god's sake, call the police," she shouted. "Call the police."

The man beckoned his wife and she raced back home. From within her house, the man could hear Veronica screaming, "You can kill me but you will not influence the kids anymore." Her words were as clear as a running stream. "And you won't stay here, you fucking junkie. Get out of my house. I am appalled with myself for having loved you."

The voices changed from clear to muffled as the man pressed his ear against the door, trying to decipher what was being said. Marcos had backed off, now supporting himself on the kitchen table. He was the one out of breath but Veronica was the one lying in a ball on the floor, in pain and in agony.

"So you don't want me anymore, then?" His words came out one at a time as he tried to control his breathing. "You don't love me anymore."

Veronica replied calmly, not because she was but because she had no more energy to shout. "You're crazy. Out of your mind. No one will ever love you when they find out who you really are." She climbed sheepishly to her feet and slowly walked to the front door. "You're nothing but a worthless drug addict," she added. "A coward that had everything then threw it all away, including his own family," she concluded, as she opened the door.

The man took a step inside the house. "Are you alright, Veronica?" he asked with a hint of concern.

Veronica's back was arched, her forearm holding her painful stomach. A thin line of blood had trickled from the corner of her mouth. "I'm fine," she reassured him. "Thank you, Mr Arlete."

"Ermm, Veronica. You appear to have a tooth missing." Mr Arlete pointed to the equivalent tooth in his own set, using his index finger. Veronica poked around with her tongue until she found the vacated cavity. "I best call an ambulance," he said.

"No," she insisted, taking him by the arm to prevent him from leaving. "That won't be necessary, thank you. I'm fine, really." Mr Arlete nodded. "I would very much appreciate it if you would stay here until he leaves."

"Yes, of course," he agreed. "My wife, though, has called for the police."

"Has she?" She turned around and took a step forward. "You hear that, Marcos?" she said. "The police are on their way. I'd take off if I were you. With your previous police record, they are likely to throw the key away when they get hold of you."

He did not require his wife's invitation. He was already on his way to the door. As he approached the threshold, he stopped for a moment, looking straight ahead. Without a single word or a glimpse of his wife, he continued his exit with the puppy sitting in his arms. He walked briskly along the garden path and then vanished.

Mr Arlete watched him leave until he disappeared beyond the garden greenery. He looked at Veronica. "You really need to see a doctor."

"No, I'm fine," she promised. "I just need a shower and to clean up this mess."

He gently guided her into the house and closed the door. "Go and clean yourself up. I'll make a start here until the maid comes back."

She undressed herself gently in front of the large mirror that hung from the wall, addressing each injury as they appeared. She didn't look too bad, she thought, except her face that had a nasty bruise on her left cheek, a small cut above her left eye and a larger cut on her bottom lip. How would she explain the injuries to her work colleges?

The humiliation by Marcos would soon spread as gossip throughout the school and she was sure that there would be some awkward questions asked by the headteachers. She considered the option of going long-term sick until the marks faded but that would mean no salary and the bills needed paying and the children fed. Her missing tooth would not be a problem, though. She could get an emergency appointment and a temporary tooth implanted while the permanent replacement was being made. She would call the dentist after her shower.

Veronica stood naked, checking for marks on her body in the mirror. A large bruise was growing beneath her ribs and another was in the centre of her stomach. That one hurt considerable. It was already a colour of deep purple and she hoped that it would not get any worse. There didn't appear to be any more significant marks. As she scanned the ugly contusions, she said out aloud, "Oh god. Did I come in to this world just to be someone else's punch bad? Not even a prostitute deserves this kind of treatment."

She completed her shower and hand washed the splashes of blood from the side of the bath. Satisfied that the evidence of her brutal attack was cleared, she put on her thick white bathrobe. She felt a sharp pain in her left breast but could see no injury. There were no marks underneath either as she lifted her breast with her right hand but pain could still be felt. Discarding it quickly as a bruise waiting to shine, she closed the robe and fastened it tightly but gently with its cord.

Mr Arlete had already left and, as she looked out of the living room window, could see that he was talking to the police by the garden gates, gesturing occasionally with his hands. She suspected that he was feeding them some fake story to keep them from knocking on her door. *What a nice man*, she thought.

He always went the full distance to help Veronica and the children in any way that he could. It wasn't his prerogative and never had been but he was always there, at hand if needed. Sometimes, she felt that he fancied her as she had seen him looking at her, sometimes from safety of his own home, despite the fact he was a married man. But she didn't hold it against him. He was far too nice a man to hold any malice.

Veronica closed the flower designed net curtain and wandered in to the kitchen. The maid had returned from her jaunt to the school, the children now safely in the hands of their teachers. She went to speak but Veronica held up her hand to halt what she wanted to say. Instead, she offered her a smile and began to fold the ironed clothing. The kitchen had been tidied up and cleaned of blood that had gathered on the floor by the table. As she made herself a cup of organic strawberry and cucumber green tea, the maid, carrying the washing basket of fresh clothes, adjourned upstairs.

Veronica carefully poured the boiling water directly on to the teabag that was sitting impatiently in the mug. She sat at the kitchen table, straightening one of the chairs as she did. She knew that the children would have to adjust to the absence of their father, who was planning to settle in Vitoria.

They had already begun to accept it, with the invaluable help of Ana Beatriz, but the events of the past two days were a terrible setback. How much damage had been done was currently unclear but Veronica hoped and prayed that it would be limited. She didn't care about herself; she had endured so much physical and mental pain from Marcos and beyond and, to her, that was just the norm. Business as usual. It was the children that she had to protect and she didn't want to see them turn into gun carrying gangsters, women beaters or wife or husband abusers.

From that day on, Marcos had no contact with them or Veronica. The only time they saw each other was in passing on the street or over the park. He would perhaps exchange a few words with his children before going to do whatever he planned to do. He never had a gift for them and he never ever said those words that were expected from a father; I love you.

To him, his own children were just acquaintances or kids that belonged to other families. Just another person living in Vitoria. Veronica would hide in some secluded corner, like a fox from its predators, if she saw him heading her way. It was an awful way to live but necessary, to keep the peace and to rebuild.

Time came and went and over the following five years, Veronica barely saw him. The children saw him maybe half a dozen times a year. With him no longer around, they all lead peaceful and quiet lives full of happiness and solitude, with the children growing into respectful, dependable and reliable adults.

The divorce petition logged by Veronica nearly two years ago through Notice by Publication had been heard by the court, even though he had not attended any of the hearings. The divorce was therefore granted, with no contesting and with the papers signed, she was at last a free woman. Over her long suffering years, she had lost many battles with Marcos but it was her that had finally won the war.

None of the children were affected or even concerned by it. They had long ago come to accept the inevitable and knew that one day it would happen. Out of all the five children, it was Junior that found it hardest to let go.

Now, at fifteen years old, he sometimes went to the town, hoping to bump in to his father. He would only do it occasionally and most of the time it would fail but this particular time, he saw him, exiting an off-licence, holding a bottle of vodka. His clothes were dirt stained and untidy, his hair long and unhealthy and was in desperate need of a shave. Junior, at first glance, didn't recognise him. It was his stumble into the street bin that first caught his attention.

After exchanging a few sentences, he asked Junior if he'd like to come and live with him at his apartment, as he was his only son. He also moaned and complained that he was very lonely and that it wasn't fair that Veronica had all the children. Junior subsequently told his mother about the meeting, which filled her with great concern and anxiety. He was just entering his adolescence and was at the stage where he was vulnerable and impressionable. The way he expressed himself and his clear excitement told her that his father's offer was being taken very seriously.

Veronica told her son that it was not going to happen while he was still underage and classed as a child. She explained that they knew nothing of the life he lead and the people he might be mixing with. They didn't even know where he lived. She did not want fifteen years of hard work undone, converting him from a decent, loving boy into who knows what. She told him it was OK to visit on the odd occasion but he was never to spend the night. Junior did not tell his mother that he often scouted the streets of the town, looking for him and he made no promises to her in reply to what she expected of him.

The seeds of his intentions had been planted. He was growing into an independent, free-thinking individual, capable of making his own decisions and acting on them but still too young and inexperienced to comprehend the consequences. His mother went ballistic with worry when he didn't return home one night.

In panic, she searched the town streets for him without success. He was nowhere to be seen. It was dark and the middle of the night and she feared for his safety. She found herself passing the local police station on Merzia Street and rushed inside.

After reporting the incident and supplying the officers with a photo, the police chief ordered a car to cruise the neighbourhood where Marcos may have been living. Veronica went with them, sitting in the back, carefully scrutinising the few people that were out and about at 4 o'clock in the morning. It was on the forecourt of the twenty-four hour petrol station that they saw him, carrying a plastic bag containing two rattling bottles of alcohol.

The police car pulled up, parking on the pavement and Veronica opened the door and hurriedly climbed out.

"Junior," she called out, running towards him. He stopped at his brisk walk and turned round. "What are you doing here, son?" she asked with anger and relief in her voice. "I've been worried sick, looking for you all night. Where have you been?"

Junior briefly diverted his eyes from his mother to the two police officers alighting from their vehicle. He returned his gaze. "Mum, I'm not coming home with you." He spoke with considerable calm and control. "I am going to live with dad from now on," he continued. "You have all my sisters with you and he has no one, mum. No one at all."

She squinted in the darkness as she looked at him, the petrol station providing some limited light. He appeared different somehow, not significantly but enough for her to notice. His eyes looked bloodshot, as if he'd been violently rubbing them through lack of sleep. He was subtly swaying from side to side, desperately trying to hide his unstable sense of balance and despite his calm demeanour, his speech was slow and intermittently slurred.

Veronica's sister Ines once told her that intuition was a gift that all women had but that was not needed here. The alcohol he was carrying in the bag helped answer her query but was it just that? She feared that his father may have introduced him to his world of drugs and gambling and was grooming him to never return home. With exams looming on the horizon as well, his schooling was guaranteed to suffer irreparable damage.

Veronica turned to the police officer that was spinning the car keys on his finger in an orchestra of clinking, out-of-tune notes. "I can't leave my son here. He needs to come home," she told him. "He needs to go to school to study for his exams in four months' time."

The policeman stopped spinning the keys and popped them in his trouser pocket. "Madam, he is at home. He's with his father," he replied. "As a fifteen-year-old, he can choose who he wants to live with."

"He's still a child, for god's sake. Still at school and still under my guardianship." Her calmness was forsaking her. "It's my choice, not his."

"Please keep you voice down. There are people still asleep if you hadn't noticed. This is Brazil, ma'am. Not Europe or America." He paused as an over modulating and incoherent voice sounded from the police radio. He beckoned his partner to attend to it. "Your son *is* old enough to decide for himself where he wants to live and has done exactly that. Now, if you want to contest it, then it'll involve the courts and from where I am standing, that is just a lost cause for you."

He placed a gentle hand on her shoulder and led her a few steps away. "Put your trust in god, ma'am. This is a very undesirable area full of criminals and drug addicts. It seems that your son has had a good education so he'll know what's right and wrong. I suggest you give him time and let him make his own choices and mistakes. If he makes a bad choice, then he will be back, I promise you."

Veronica appreciated the officers' well-rehearsed words that he'd probably said a hundred times before, words that she did not want to hear right now. She walked over to Junior, who had been watching on with great interest. She placed a hand on each of his shoulders, a tear in her eye and begged him, "Please, son. Please come home with me. You belong with me and your sisters in our beautiful house. This is not your place."

He very slowly shook his head a few times. "Go to the girls, mum," he said. "My place is now with dad. He needs me. I'll come and visit you all as much as I am able. After all, we are only forty minutes apart."

The officer took Veronica by the arm in an effort to lead her away from the scene but was unwilling to oblige. "Come on, madam," he said. "There is nothing more for you to do here."

She allowed him to gently pull her away. Junior stood motionless as she climbed into the police car and, as the car pulled away, he once again watched as his mother travelled the corridor of uncertainty, until it vanished into the darkness beyond.

The police had been very accommodating and helpful, even though the outcome was not what Veronica had hoped for. They didn't have to drive her home but perhaps they had felt sympathy for her predicament and could see how upset she was. So many officers would ignore problems like that and leave them to sort it themselves, even if it meant leaving a vulnerable lady alone on the streets at night, unless, of course, you slipped them a bribe to pay for their end-of-shift breakfast.

She arrived home just before 5 o'clock, feeling tired and emotionally drained. The children were still sleeping soundly and, in an hour, the maid would wake them up and prepare them for school. She went straight to her room, sat on the bed beside the chest of drawers, opened the top drawer and removed her bible. Veronica had been bought up as a devout Catholic and often turned to the good book in times of trouble.

Sometimes, she just held it in her hands without reading its words but this time she opened it at Psalm 23, asking god to anoint her head to help her to cope and to send her son back home and not to fall into the world of illegal drugs. She could not bear the pain of seeing her son lost to the evils of the world.

But god didn't listen. It wasn't long before he was arrested for possession of 'class A' drugs and was subsequently jailed. To help pay for their addiction, they turned to crime, robbing street revellers at night by gun point, shoplifting from supermarkets and breaking into cars. It bought in a modest illegal income but not enough to cover for the drugs that they were now snorting, smoking and injecting. Marcos enticed his son to steal from his own mother, as he knew that she wouldn't report it.

Over time, he took paintings, personal items, vases and other ceramics; anything that would fetch a price. Eventually, her chequebook went missing, using it to withdraw cash and to purchase resell-able items from shops, knowing that the bills would end up in his mother's hand. All of their illegal profits went straight to the pushers in a desperate attempt to stay in credit as their addiction blew way out of control. The danger it brought to Veronica and the children was incomprehensible. The drug dealers could turn up at her house at any time, guns in hand, demanding payment.

Junior was no longer aware of what he was doing, permanently high on cocaine or preoccupied with getting his next payday. Veronica tried again and again to bring him to his senses and wake him from his nightmare but all her efforts were futile. Endless times he sought sanctuary at his mother's house, fleeing and hiding from death threats and, when he craved a fix, would take off again, not to be seen for weeks on end. She could no longer chase after him as her resolve was weakening and she knew exactly what would happen if she caught up with him.

Everything now depended on him. Only he could pull himself out of this senseless life he had created but, with a father that controlled him with a leash and as a joint addict, that possibility seemed a million miles away. Perhaps going to prison might help him get clean but was unlikely as drugs were just as easily available inside as out.

Veronica's heart sank as the realisation hit her hard. She had to let him go, for the sake of the family. Junior was no longer her son, he was long gone. He was now a slave to Satan, living in the deepest depths of hell. She wrote a list of things she had to do to close this terrible chapter in her life, one of them being that she would never visit him in jail.

She recalled visits to jail many years ago, which probably did more harm than good and she could not and would not endure that again. For months, she read the list each day until it was permanently implanted in her brain. She felt that it was the only way for her to move forward and not be stuck in limbo indefinitely. It made her cry constantly but the horrors and hardships she had lived with all her life had made her strong, resilient and unbreakable. The children would also accept one day.

Chapter Six

The days quickly turned into weeks and then months, eventually into years. The children had all grown four years older and Veronica still lived in that beautiful house up on the hill. Her two part-time jobs were still in full bloom, with her freelance beauty job now an independent business. It had grown rapidly in its early days but had slowed after a year.

New customers still arrived, joining the congregation of her regulars and, as its clientele increased, she had to eventually employ and train new staff, eight in total. They moved to their own premises but continued to pay royalties to its original founder, the owner of the salon on Teixa Boulevard.

She often thought about Junior but it no longer delivered pain. She hadn't seen nor heard from him or Marcos for over four years and wondered if they even still lived in Vitoria. It was possible, of course, that he (or they) was still incarcerated but wherever they were, they had left her and the children alone. Nobody in the house spoke of them or asked questions, which Veronica appreciated as she wanted to leave it in the past and let the sleeping dog lie.

As the children were now older and becoming independent and with a workforce she could rely on, Veronica, at last, found that she had more time to go out and have fun and to enjoy valuable time with her eldest, Ana Beatriz. They arranged to have lunch at a beach restaurant that commanded beautiful views of the bay and the rugged cliffs to the left. An armada of boats populated the bay, from two berth sailing boats to private yachts and, on the horizon, a cruise ship slowly crawled by. The stunning view would grace any picture post-card.

They enjoyed a banquet of fresh seafood that had been caught in the bay by the local fishermen including oysters, crab and scallops, washed down with a bottle of white wine. Ana Beatriz was one of their many regular customers and frequented the restaurant often, usually at the weekend. If it was available, she'd always sit at table eleven as she rather liked the waiter (Charlie as he was known but not his real name), sharing the odd flirt with him and indulging in a cheeky conversation when business was quiet. He often sent her a smile or a wink as he strolled past her, tray in hand as he served other diners.

As Veronica poured the last of the wine into the empty glasses, Ana Beatriz tapped her mother on her shoe, as if she were playing footsie and gestured with her head as he headed toward them. He had no trays expertly balanced on his palms and no filled glasses clasped in his fingers. As he approached their table, he looked at her sweetly before greeting her. "Good afternoon, Ana," he said. He never used her double name. "Forgive the intrusion of your meal," he continued apologetically, addressing them both. "This is for you, madam."

Charlie handed a folded piece of paper to Veronica, looked her in the eyes and bowed slightly. As he left, he cheekily winked at Ana Beatriz.

"What's that, mum?" she enquired, watching her as she unfolded it.

On the 'Romulo's Restaurant' headed note paper was an elegantly handwritten message in blue ink. The message was short, sweet and very intriguing: *Please allow me to buy you both a drink to complement a lovely meal.*

"Somebody wants our attention by buying us drinks," Veronica answered. She looked around to see a well-groomed and sharply dressed man sitting at the bar, holding his half empty beer glass in the air.

"Hey, mum. That's the owner of this restaurant," Ana Beatriz told her. "He's from Portugal, I think."

Veronica didn't hear her daughter's words as she was transfixed with his handsome, Iberian looks. A thick, black moustache complimented his dark hair and brown eyes. His physic suggested that he worked out in a gym regularly and his polished, shiny shoes twinned perfectly with his designer pinstripe suit.

He confidently hopped off the bar stool, adjusted his tie and moved toward them. Veronica watched his every move as he drew nearer; oozing style and panache. Full of grace.

"Hello, ladies," he said. "I'm Romulo. I am the owner of this restaurant," he proudly commented. "Allow me to buy you something to drink."

Veronica stood up and shook his hand. "Hi, I'm Nica," she nervously said. "And this is my daughter, Ana Beatriz."

She remained in her seat but gave him one of her warm smiles.

Romulo gestured to Charlie, who was standing anonymously in the background. "What can I get you both?" he asked.

"Thank you," Veronica said. "I'd love a sambuca."

"Me too," Ana Beatriz agreed.

Charlie nodded and headed to the bar.

"Unfortunately, I can't join you, but I just wanted to say that you have a stunning-looking daughter and I would like to think that she will look as good as you when reaches your age," he paused a moment as he digested what he had just said. "Did that come out right?"

Veronica giggled at his compliment. "Yes, it came out just fine, thank you."

Charlie returned with the drinks, standing proudly on a silver tray. He carefully placed on the table before departing.

"Enjoy your sambucas," Romulo said to Veronica. "I have to go now, as I have business to take care of. I hope you don't think it is too forward of me but may I ask you for your telephone number. Perhaps you will allow me to take you out for dinner one evening. But not here," he said with a smile on his face. "There are plenty of good eateries in town."

Veronica felt a mixture of hesitancy and embarrassment. Not because she had been invited out but at the suddenness of it all. She was not expecting it and caught her totally by surprise. Before she could offer a response, Ana Beatriz nodded her head and raised her eyebrows in approval, which was normally a good omen.

"OK," she said without any real conviction. She picked her purse up from the table and removed one of her business cards from the pouch and handed it to him.

He quickly glanced at it before tucking it into the top pocket of his blazer. Without a word but just a smile, he walked away. Veronica watched him until he disappeared through a door behind the bar. "I didn't feel comfortable giving him my number," she told her daughter, who had already drained half of her complimentary drink.

"Oh, mum," she replied. "It's time you found a nice man to join your life and he seems a nice guy. You are a beautiful lady and you deserve someone special to make you happy."

She raised her shot glass once again and finished what little sambuca remained. "Mum, you have drifted from part-time relationships to seedy affairs over the past four years and none of them have bought you any real happiness, have they?" She started to rotate her glass with her thumb and index finger, as if she were trying to screw it in into the table. "All I'm saying is give him a chance. If you don't like him, then it's no big deal." She pointed towards the horizon, where dark clouds were starting to gather. "Looks like rain."

Veronica looked up. "Hmm," she agreed as she watched a fishing boat slowly cruising to its mooring space. Its horn sounded loudly, informing the harbour master of its intentions. "He probably won't call me, anyway," she commented.

"He'll call you, you can be rest assured of that," Ana Beatriz promised her. "I saw how you looked at him, mum. Talk about instant attraction." She smiled at her mother, who was contemplating whether to indulge in her drink. "Anyway, you shouldn't be so pessimistic, otherwise everything will just end up with disappointment." She looked down at the inviting drink, sitting lonely on the table. "Are you going to drink that, mum?"

She picked up the tempting treat and emptied it with a single swig. It caused her to mildly cough as the alcohol made its presence felt. She set the glass down gently on the table. "Come on, we'd best be on our way," she said, noticing the dark skies in the distance approaching ever closer.

A flash of lightening beautifully lit up the horizon, reflected artistically in the flat, calm sea, followed by a deep but distant clap of thunder.

Veronica placed her purse in her handbag as Ana Beatriz slipped a five $R note under a saucer for Charlie's impeccable service and headed for the taxi rank.

"Whose turn is it to pay for the taxi?" Ana Beatriz asked.

"Ha-ha," came Veronica's sarcastic laugh. "It's your turn but I know it will come out of my purse."

As Charlie collected his tip, he watched the two of them amble down the short alleyway that led on to the main road. Moments later, they were gone.

Ana Beatriz had been right, as usual. Her intuition was like a superpower, a sixth sense that she had somehow managed to develop and often used it to her advantage. Or was it that she just had prior knowledge and knew something that her mother didn't? Either way, Romulo did the phone that very evening, just as she was preparing for bed. They chatted for a good hour about everything and nothing, feeling their way in their newfound friendship.

To her surprise, he spoke frankly about his restaurant and the fact that it was struggling and was very close to failing. He had opened it some three years ago and at first, it did well. Very well, in fact. It was the first seafood restaurant of its kind to open in Vitoria and the public loved what it had to offer. After just a few months, Romulo began working on opening a second in Rio but it never materialised.

With the rising of interest rates and unemployment, his business began to suffer badly. Not just him either. The high street saw a number of shops close and some of the properties still remain vacant to this day. Sixteen months after his grand opening, he began to use his own money to keep it afloat, to the complete horror of his accountant. And now the business had left him almost broke, except for a few thousand dollars he had put into his Portuguese bank account. That was his emergency stash in the event of a major catastrophe and of course, bent policeman and kidnappers, they wouldn't accept credit cards.

He told Veronica he had done a lot of soul searching recently and was seriously considering a return to Lisbon. He had no interest in staying in Brazil to work for a company that paid him low wages that left him with no money to buy food after the monthly bills were paid.

For as long as he could remember, he had always been his own boss with various different business ventures, not always legal but, nevertheless, his own. He insisted he could always make money some way or another, even if it was a fruit stall on the side street. His restaurant was his biggest challenge to date and he felt devastated it was going under. Veronica reassured him that although that was the case, he may well have regretted it if he hadn't given it a try and that he was still young enough to rebuild.

It was getting close to midnight when they ended the call. Veronica would love to have continued but she had clients to beautify in the morning and then an afternoon shift awaited her at the school. She felt well within her comfort zone, talking to him.

He was happy to take the lead and happy to pick and choose the subject to chat about. His company felt so natural to her, with no uncomfortable pauses and no limitations to what was said. She had invited him to come to her house for dinner, arranged for Saturday week and was very happy to accept her kind offer. In the meantime, he asked her to accompany him to the cafe in the park on Friday afternoon where they could enjoy a cappuccino, watching the tennis matches. She agreed and this date led to another four more and all before Saturday's dinner date had even arrived.

As they enjoyed the atmosphere of the tennis on a warm early evening, a figure sat on a bench on the far side of the courts, the peak of his baseball cap sitting low on his forehead, partially covering his face. Through the tennis court fences, he sat there watching them from a distance as they laughed and smiled together, holding each other's hands in their own private little world.

He wanted to walk over and greet his mother but he didn't like the look of the man that she sat with. The frustration he felt left a trail of anger in its wake, anger that he had so desperately tried to control over the years. He rose from the wooden bench and stood like a statue, watching them for a few more moments. He then turned and began to slowly walk away. As he reached the public pathway, Junior adjusted his baseball cap.

Although Veronica had seen Romulo a number of times over the past week, she still felt apprehension and nervous about tonight's dinner date. She had given the maid the evening off, who took advantage of the free time to visit her sister. Veronica wanted to prepare the dinner herself to make the evening even more special and to show off her cooking skills. She spent over two hours making herself look beautiful and wore a blue, knee length summer dress decorated with embroidered flowers. After a final inspection in her full length bedroom mirror, she said to herself, "Wow, you never looked so good!"

She had prepared the dining table elegantly and with precision, as a restaurant owner would expect and appreciate. There were two opened bottles of wine, one red and the other white, both sitting in their own ice buckets together with a bottle of sambuca waiting to be opened with after dinner coffee. She smiled at the results of her hard work with complete satisfaction and felt sure that Romulo would be proud of her housekeeping skills. It was fast approaching 7 o'clock, so she unlocked and opened the front door in anticipation of his imminent arrival.

That's when she saw him, standing next to the open gate. At first, she did not recognise who it was as her brain refused to accept the vision that stood before her eyes. He was still wearing the same baseball cap he had on at the park. Her first thought was to scream at him to go away but common sense advised her otherwise. She couldn't understand her own feelings. There should have been joy and happiness flowing through her heart but she didn't feel that. Was it the shock of seeing him after four years? Or was it something more sinister?

She descended the porch steps, cautiously and hesitantly walking the garden path. He just stood there with his hand resting on the gatepost. No smile appeared on his lips, no excitement engulfed him, no arms lifted in the offer of a hug. He just stood there, as if frozen in time. The short walk seemed to take an eternity. As she drew ever closer, Romulo appeared behind him, carrying a large bouquet of flowers, dressed impeccably as always.

With apprehension growing, she briefly glanced at him before returning her gaze to Junior. He still stood in the gateway, not yielding to the new arrival, denying him any access.

"Junior," she exclaimed. "What are you doing here?"

He said nothing in return as he turned to face Romulo, squaring up to him with eyes full of intimidation. Romulo stood in complete surprise and shock. As a long serving restaurateur, he was trained to expect the unexpected, but he never saw this coming. He offered his hand in friendship but was ignored. "Hi, Junior," he said as he lowered his hand. "I'm Romulo. It's nice to meet you."

"I know who you are," he replied coldly and without feeling.

Veronica stepped forward. "Romulo, why don't you go into the house and put the flowers in water?" she suggested. "And help yourself to a drink. If you fancy some wine, you'll find some on the dinner table."

Romulo gestured to Junior to allow him to pass but he stood his ground. He felt no fear from the youngster but a lot of confusion.

Once again, Veronica intervened. "Junior, let him pass, please."

It took him a few more seconds before he stepped aside and Romulo confidently strolled through the gate. "I'll get you a drink as well, dear," he said to Veronica as he passed.

She briefly watched as he and the flowers headed to the house, then turned to her son. "It's wonderful to see you, son," she said. He looked ill, as if he hadn't been eating properly and not caring for himself. She quickly assessed that he had lost weight and was in desperate need of a shower and shave. His clothing was no better. "Don't I get a cuddle, then?"

"You've got a nerve, you really have," He spoke with total disregard and without an ounce of love. "You destroyed dad, completely. You broke his heart and now you act like nothing has happened." He raised his arm and pointed at the house. "And now you have a fancy man, wearing a poxy suit with a matching tie."

"I have never hidden anything from you," she firmly stated. "I told you everything that happened four years ago, even though you were still young. I left nothing out at all. What has happened has happened. It was a long time ago and I'm not going to go through it all again." She held her tongue for a moment, allowing him to digest her words. "It's in the past and that's where it's going to stay."

"I saw you at the park last week," he told her. "At the tennis match. You and your fancy man. Having such a wonderful time while dad continues to suffer. I saw you with him at the art gallery. And I watched you eating at the new Chinese restaurant a couple of days ago, as well." He shook his head. "You have such a short memory."

"Have you been following me?" she asked with utter surprise. A nod of his head was his answer. "Why didn't you come and say hello? Why all the sneaking around? Why all the cloak and dagger stuff?" She paused but no answer was forthcoming. "I'm your mother, for god's sake. You don't need to hide in the shadows."

Her last statement caught his attention. "A mother, yes," he shouted. "And a wife as well. Two roles that you are unable to fulfil."

An uncomfortable silence fell upon them. The realisation beat at her hard like a punch from a heavyweight boxer. Marcos never told him that they had divorced. She knew that he used everyone to get what he wanted and suspected that he'd kept it quiet to keep him on the side, to keep the sympathy and support rolling in.

"Oh, Junior," she said apologetically. "I'm so sorry. He didn't tell you, did he? We're divorced, a long time ago. Well, over a year."

"No, you're lying," he said, shaking his head. "He *would* have told me."

"I'm not lying to you, Junior. I have the divorce papers inside if you want to see them."

"Why wouldn't he tell me?"

Veronica shrugged her shoulders. "It's a simple answer," she said. "He didn't tell because he's your father and it's what he does." Junior wanted to look his mother in the eye but found it a difficult prospect. "Why don't you come into the house and eat dinner with us," she continued. "There's plenty there. And if you feel comfortable, you can take a shower and I'll run your clothes through the washing machine."

"No. No, thank you," he said. "I don't want to impose." He turned away to leave but she caught him by the arm.

"You're definitely not imposing," Veronica insisted. "Come on, walk with me."

He said nothing as she led him up the garden path, through the open door and into the living room. Glasses knocking together told them that Romulo was in the kitchen.

"As you can see, dinner is ready," she told him. "Why don't you go to see Romulo and make your peace with him and I'll dish up the food?"

It wasn't his ideal scenario but he reluctantly agreed. He didn't want to make any peace with him. He didn't want his friendship, didn't want his advice and he definitely didn't want him as a step dad. Junior only wanted one thing for him.

Slowly, he walked through the kitchen door, swinging it shut with one hand as he did so.

As she prepared the vegetables for dinner, Veronica suddenly heard a commotion from the kitchen. Slightly raised voices at first and then the brash sounds of breaking crockery, followed by an agonising scream. She raced through the door to be greeted by the two of them fighting. Romulo had a large injury to his upper arm that was bleeding heavily, seeping through the arm of his blazer. That's when she noticed the knife in Junior's hand. He was slowly inching towards him, knife held up aloft in defiance, as Romulo backed away.

"Stop it, Junior," Veronica cried out. "Stop it, now. Put the knife down."

Junior appeared not to hear his mother's plea as he continued to move forward. Smeared blood was clearly visible on the blade as it glistened in the bright setting sun. She quickly thrust towards him, pushing him to the tiled floor. He landed on his side, sending the knife spiralling from his hand, coming to rest somewhere beneath the washing machine. He rolled on to his side but did not rise. He did not appear to have any injuries.

Veronica took out a kitchen cloth from one of the drawers and wrapped it gently around the seeping wound, tying a knot tightly, causing Romulo to wince at the sharp pain. The arm of his suit was soaked in blood. Despite the events unfolding before her, she was remarkably calm and expressed no panic.

"You need to go to hospital," she explained, as she patched him up. "It's a nasty injury. You're bleeding an awful lot."

They left Junior unconscious on the cold floor as they left. Veronica figured that he'd be OK as he had no physical injuries, whereas Romulo was a more pressing case. They arrived at the hospital in good time and was attended too very quickly. The nurse cut the arms off his suit and shirt and subsequently began to clean and disinfect the gash before inserting the five stitches needed to stem the flow of blood. His pain was constant and persistent, causing him to groan with a face of agony.

Following the successful but quick procedure, the nurse finally gave him a small injection of morphine to dull the pain and dutifully sent them on their way. Romulo promised to return in a day or two to complete the paperwork.

They exited the hospital grounds and stood by the entrance, awaiting a taxi to take them home. Veronica took his (good) hand and sadly said, "We should stop off at the police station and report this."

"No." His response was immediate. "No need for that."

"The nurse is right. We should report it by law." She was adamant it needed to be done. "He can't be allowed to attack someone and stab them with a knife, especially you and then go unpunished."

"It's no big deal, dear," he assured her. "He will hopefully regret what he has done in time and offer some sort of apology."

Did he really believe that? Probably not, but it was reassuring and Veronica needed that.

"Anyway, you have suffered enough, so why prolong that? Let me tell you something, OK? I have a lifetime of experience and, for everything that I have seen and gone through, I'm telling you that your son is a lost cause. Just hopeless. He might, one day, return to reality and the wondrous life that he is wasting, if he is lucky enough to meet a good, honest and very patient lady that is willing to guide his heart in the right direction."

He raised his hand to hail a taxi that was alighting a passenger from across the road. "You can't watch him forever. He is an adult and will do what he wants to. If you respect him, you will let him go. It's all in god's hands now. Only he can show him the road to recovery."

The taxi pulled away and crawled slowly across the road, halting briefly to give way to a cyclist. It parked up beside them and Romulo opened the rear door for Veronica to climb in. She knew that he was right in his comments. He spoke a lot of sense but it wasn't that easy to just 'let him go.'

Over the past four years she had done exactly that but she badly suffered, thinking and worrying about him every day, wondering whether he was still in jail and if he was still an addict. She may not have seen him in all that time but he was always there, in her mind and thoughts, so she had never truly abandoned him. He lived locally and as today proved, he could return to her life to hurt and torture her, anytime he wanted.

As the taxi exited the rank to join the queue of traffic at the main junction, a thought came to her that heavily caught her attention 'Perhaps now is the right time for me to leave.'

A great deal happened over the following three months. Romulo's restaurant was sold well below its valued price, Veronica resigned from her position at the school to concentrate on her beauty business and, she also hadn't seen Junior at all during that period. She even stopped making secretive enquiries about him.

She still thought about him occasionally but somehow managed to program herself to switch it off when needed. It was the only way to move forward that had any success.

His plans to return to Portugal were well underway, with just a few loose ends to take care of, one of those being his partner. For many weeks, he wasn't sure how to handle it. He loved her dearly and wanted her to go with him but with such a large family rooted firmly in Brazil, he knew how difficult it would be for her to leave it all behind. The dilemma tormented his thoughts constantly and often kept him awake at night. A positive decision had to be made either way and he had far too much love for her to just disappear without a word. He needed to be strong and forceful and confident in his choice for the future.

It was a hot, beautiful Sunday afternoon while walking in the park that he asked her to marry him and join him in Portugal. To his complete surprise, she accepted his proposal straight away, with no consideration needed at all. He suggested that he leave first to arrange all that was needed in preparation for her arrival and, in the meantime, she would be able to conclude her arrangements before departing.

A window of three months was his offering but she felt that she may need more time to get everything done, so a compromise of four months was agreed.

With the children all grown and leading secure and steady lives, Veronica felt that if it was ever going to happen, then this was the right time. Ana Beatriz was already a mother of a two-year-old boy and in a strong relationship, Luciana also had motherly duties with a son of less than a year, Isabela was engaged to be married and studying Economics in Sao Paulo and Anna Luiza was a student, now at sixteen years old.

All the girls were level-headed, intelligent and sensible and Veronica knew that they would all be happy and stable, even though they felt sadness that their mother would soon be leaving to live in Europe.

Her biggest worry was Junior. Well, not really worry, more like mild concern. All of those negative emotions that had plagued her for so long were no longer in residence. She felt it her duty to, at some stage, have one final chat with him before the time came that it could no longer happen. She knew exactly where to find him and, at the appropriate time, would pay him a visit. She needed to tell him of her plans to leave and express upon him, his need to repent and reform. It was possible that he already knew, as it wasn't exactly a secret but if he did, then there had been no word or visit.

Romulo's departure date soon arrived and, with all loose ends tied up and his bags packed, Veronica and the girls accompanied him to the airport. She felt great sadness but, at the same time, excessive excitement. Her future looked bright and promising and couldn't wait for it all to begin. After checking in his bags, they joined the queue at passport control.

He tightly hugged his fiancée for a few moments before releasing her. "Don't look so sad," he observed. "It's just a for a few months. And if you are ready before then, you can come earlier."

"I'm OK, really," she reassured him. "I will try my best to get it all done as quickly as I am able."

He smiled and nodded with approval, then turned to the girls, who had all been looking on. He kissed each of them on the cheek, accompanied by a quick cuddle. "Don't forget girls," he told them. "You are all welcome to come and visit whenever you want to." His offer was much appreciated by them. "Don't be a stranger, any of you."

There was a mixture of nodding heads and mumbles of 'OK'.

He cuddled Veronica one last time, gently kissed her on the lips and gave her one of his trademark handsome smiles. They watched him as he approached the officer sitting in a glass protected booth. He handed his passport to the uniformed man, who studied it for a minute, flipping through its numerous pages, before returning it. After passing through, he turned around and raised his hand high in the air and gave them all one last wave. The girls responded with cries of 'goodbye' and 'see you' and seconds later, he was gone.

His departure left an empty, lonely, black void in Veronica's life. It had only been a few days and she missed him terribly. It was a real struggle to motivate herself to do anything and she spent less and less time at her salon. Any problems that occurred were usually resolved with a phone call with her assistant and harsh words like 'Deal with it yourself' or 'Get a grip. You can handle it'.

Veronica had endless tasks to complete with very little time to complete them in and she didn't want unnecessary complications holding her up. She was eager to organise everything quickly but responsibly so that she could leave as soon as possible. That's all she wanted to do, nothing else interested her and she knew that the salon would soon be no longer part of her life.

That afternoon, she went to visit Ines at her house. They hadn't seen each other for a while and she was eager to catch up with everything. There was also business to discuss. It was a particularly hot afternoon with the sun beating down mercilessly on the residents of Vitoria with not a single fluffy cloud to be seen. They elected to sit inside at the dinner table, beneath the ceiling fan with a jug of cool orange juice.

Ines dropped ice cubes in Veronica's drink with a plop and placed it carefully on a cardboard beer mat. "How are the girls coping with your imminent departure?" she politely enquired, sipping her ice-cold juice. Ice cubes collided together with a crescendo of out-of-tune notes.

"Yeah, they are fine, sis," she promised her. "I have full support from them all and they are happy that I am taking on this new challenge."

"That's good. I hate the thought that even one of them was unhappy."

"No worries there," Veronica said, stirring her drink with a plastic straw. "I want to talk about the salon with you. As you know, I'm not going to close it. My assistant, Ingrid, is going to take control and fully run it. You know Ingrid, right? You've met her before."

Ines quickly nodded her head. "Yes, we've met a few times. I think your business is in good hands there. You can trust her."

"She's been with me a long time and she's my friend. I haven't treated her very well recently, to be honest. I must go and see her and apologise." She sipped her drink, using the straw. "The plan I have is very simple," she explained. "Each month, she will send me forty percent of the profits through bank transfer. Ten percent will also be transferred to a bank account I've opened for Anna Luiza. I'd really appreciate it if you would keep an eye on her and make sure that she is alright." Ines gestured in agreement. "The money going into her account should only be used in an emergency, so hopefully it will build up over time."

"Good idea," Ines agreed. "It seems like you have put a lot of thought into this. What you are doing is very brave and you could have easily got sidetracked."

"I still haven't spoken to Junior. He still doesn't know anything," Veronica said, pondering. "Well, I assume he doesn't know. I really need to get this unpleasant task over and done with."

"Yes, you should. Would you like me to come with you?"

"No thanks. That won't be necessary. It's my job and mine alone."

It was a good three hours later that Veronica arrived home and, to her shock, she saw Junior sitting on the porch steps, his arms resting on his knees.

"Hello, Junior," she greeted him. "What are you doing here?"

"Where have you been?" he questioned. "I've been waiting here for ages. And don't tell me you've been at the salon because I checked."

She sat next to him on the steps, leaving a significant gap between them. "I'm glad you are here. There is something I need to tell you."

"Hmm, I was wondering if you had summoned up the courage."

"What do you mean?" she asked hesitantly.

"I know exactly what you want to tell me." His tone was cold and very uninviting. "Ines told me a couple of weeks ago."

"Told you what?"

"That you are going to live in Portugal soon. When were you going to tell me?"

She paused as she watched her neighbour pass by on the street. He sent her a warm, friendly wave. "I've had a lot to do recently but I would have gotten round to it, eventually." She could not believe that her own sister could betray her. They had been so close for so long and then she had the audacity to go behind her back. It infuriated her to the core.

"You're a liar," he insisted. "You weren't going to tell me. It took your loving and trustworthy sister to do it."

"Junior, I am leaving in a few days, and I don't want to spend my last precious hours arguing with you. We have had a lifetime of confrontation, rows, fights and shouting matches. Enough is enough." She took a deep breath to repel her rising anger. "I just wanted to say, please stay out of trouble. Find yourself a job and settle down with a good woman. You cannot run from the law forever. You are an adult so behave like one. Soon, I won't be around anymore to bail you out when you get in to trouble again. Lead a good, law-abiding life otherwise one day, they will lock you up forever."

Junior rose to his feet, descended the steps and turned around. He tilted his head to one side slightly and looked her directly in the eyes. "When was the last time you told me that you loved me, mum?" he simply said. "When was the last time you told your *son* how proud you were of him?" He arched his mouth downwards in clear disappointment and gently shook his head. "From my recollection, the answer is never. I have never heard those words from you."

He turned his back and confidently walked away, for the last time, along the garden path. Veronica took a few deep breaths as she watch his image grow smaller until he eventually vanished from her vision.

Chapter Seven

Between eight of them, it took just under two days to completely clear the house of all their belongings. Veronica and the girls, together with their two friendly neighbours and their son, proved to be a very efficient team, working as one to remove the furniture, electrical appliances, paintings, ornaments and all of their personal possessions. Some of the items were placed in storage while others were either sold off, found new homes, went to the girls' apartments or merely made their way to the tip. The dish washer however, was donated to the neighbours as a thank you for their invaluable help.

The house was still in perfect condition, as it was when they moved in all those years ago. Considering how much they had accumulated over the years, Veronica finished with just two small suitcases of clothes, jewellery and a few poignant mementoes to take with her to her new life.

And now, with the house that she loved living in just an empty shell, she stayed at Ines for her final day. Even though she had badly let her down, she was still her sister and loved her dearly and appreciated her offer when it came. It was the ideal scenario for her anyway, as she didn't know when they'd see each other again, so spending her last day with her was always the right thing to do.

Ines, though, was unable to see her off at the airport due to work commitments, so it was just Anna Luiza. After a long hug, some emotional words and a few tears, they said their goodbyes. And now, sitting on the plane, her head resting on the window, watching the baggage handlers bustling about their business, her mind buzzed like a power generator in overdrive.

She was exhausted but she couldn't rest. Junior constantly entered her mind and last night, she had prayed that god would give him divine guidance and lead him along the yellow brick road to happiness and joy. She also pondered the life that awaited her in an alien country in Europe. She had sacrificed so much to be with the man she loved and she desperately needed it to work out. She hadn't known Romulo for that long, just five months or so and her actions (sincere to some, foolhardy to others) did carry an element of risk.

Positive emotions filled her heart and soul but she couldn't clear the persistent fog that hovered above them.

The ten-hour flight to Lisbon was smooth and untroubled. A few gins and tonics helped her to relax and ease her mind and, after eating a somewhat bland meal, she managed to drift off to sleep. But it wasn't for long because almost instantly, it seemed, she was awoken by a shuddering cabin as the aircraft wheels hit and briefly bounced off the runway tarmac.

Veronica opened her eyes and glanced through the scratched window, following the Portuguese scenery as it whizzed by, gradually slowing as the aircraft slammed into reverse thrust. It soon reached its taxiing speed, turning off the main runway, heading towards the vast Lisbon terminal.

She gleefully watched as rows of grounded TAP Air Portugal aircraft came into view, neatly parked in an organised fashion. Dozens of baggage trucks, pulling trailers full of bags, zigzagged expertly between the thick yellow lines, like a gathering of giant caterpillars, searching for an exit to a maze! It was an exhilarating experience for her, as she had never seen so much bustling chaos in the same moments. Vitoria airport, in comparison, was more like a child's play toy, built from Lego.

The aircraft eased to a halt as passengers unclipped their belts and began opening the overhead compartments to claim their small bags. Veronica watched them as they got in each other's way, while some stood awaiting their turn and others cursing as they were bumped and pushed by overeager and impatient travellers. She never saw the point of rushing into such a pointless exercise as the last few to claim their bags would still be alighting at the same time. *Don't they realise that the plane has a door that isn't even open yet?* she thought to herself.

As the commotion in the cabin suggested, Veronica retrieved her bag without any incidents and alighted just behind the ones that did. It brought a smile of satisfaction to her face.

Baggage claim went smoothly, even though it's the most frustrating and boring activity in the world. She waited just twenty minutes for them to appear on the noisy conveyor belt, watching them as they rotated their way towards her. The weight of the cases caused her to momentarily struggle to lift them off but was quickly assisted by a helpful gentleman looking on. She shouldered her handbag, removed her passport and tucked it into the pocket of her shorts. Next stop, passport control.

Romulo had told her that she didn't require a visa for Portugal and that they would just stamp it as a tourist visa on arrival. The length of stay, however, was the choice of the on-duty immigration officer, issuing it between one and six months. She strolled confidently to the available booth, offered the officer a smile and passed him her passport. She did not want him to see her as rude and uncouth but rather a pleasant, trustworthy and reliable visitor. After all, she was fishing for the longest visa available.

The officer did not return her greeting but carefully scanned her photo. He then looked up at her before returning to the document. A few questions followed 'How much money are you carrying?', 'Where are you staying?' and 'Are you meeting someone?' All the usual stuff! Veronica answered them clearly and concisely, in a polite and respectful manner.

The officer looked at her one last time, then, using his thumb and index finger, laid the passport flat. Using his other hand, he stamped the empty page with a dull thud, closed it and slid it back to her. He finished his transaction by saying 'Enjoy your stay.'

Veronica moved off, bags in tow and headed for customs declaration. Before passing through, she checked the issued visa. It was for three months.

She passed through customs without any problems and headed directly for the exit. As the automatic door opened, standing there immaculately dressed as ever, was Romulo, arms spread wide and grinning like a Cheshire cat.

Outside, the heavy rain fell persistently, bouncing noisily off the taxi's roof, its wipers squeaking annoyingly as they scrapped along the windscreen. Veronica folded her arms tightly as she shivered. Despite the fact that she felt cold, the driver insisted on running the air-conditioning as he puffed away on a king size cigarette.

"Cold?" Romulo asked. She smiled and nodded her head. Her smile was far from convincing. "You'll soon get used to the cooler climate here. Our summers can get just as hot as Brazil but it's only for a few months. We have four seasons here and three of them will be colder." He glanced down at her attire, wearing a thin summer t-shirt and shorts. "You're not exactly best dressed right now, but come May, it will fill more like home."

"Why is the air-con on?"

"It may be chilly for you, dear, but for the locals, it's a warm day," he explained. "Don't worry, it's only a short drive to your new home and we'll warm you up."

She watched as the streets of Lisbon passed by with curiosity in her head and excitement in her heart. It took twenty minutes before the taxi pulled up beside a tall block of flats, towering way above its neighbouring buildings.

"Here we are," Romulo said. "We are on the fourteenth floor, about two-thirds of the way up. You'll love the impressive view when you see it."

And he wasn't kidding, Veronica thought. It was indeed breathtaking, with a view that extended for many miles with the deep blue Tagus River in the far distance, on the horizon. The apartment was small and compact, with a single bedroom but a sizeable kitchen and living room. The decor, however, was degrading with faded colours, scratched paintwork and intermittent holes in the wall plaster. But overall, she thought, it was pleasant. Redecorating would be on top of the to-do list once they had settled in.

She was impressed with the kitchen size. The oven and fridge-freezer were a good size and had plenty of cupboards and draw space. Labour-saving devices sat comfortably on the worktops, including a Dulce Gusto coffee maker. Romulo knew how much she enjoyed her specialist coffee and clearly arranged it, especially for her arrival. She opened the fridge door, expecting to find it full of healthy eating foods but was amazed at its contents. Over half of the fridge was filled with beer and lager cans and very little food.

Upon opening the cupboard doors, she found more bottled alcohol, filled with vodka, gin, whisky and tequila, some of which were close to empty. She looked across at him as he stood by the window, flicking through the mail. *This wasn't normal*, she thought. *How much alcohol did he need in the flat?* And that was before she even noticed the wine stand in the corner, with a dozen or so bottles laying in its racks. She knew that the people of the Iberian Peninsula indulged in a glass of wine but this was more like stock piling. Was this a place to live or a distillery?

She called to him through the kitchen door. "Darling, I am very tired," she said. "I need to rest for a while."

He dropped the mail on to the window seal and looked up. "Of course," he replied. "You must be suffering jet lag." He glanced at his watch. "It's 11 o'clock now. Sleep all afternoon. After dinner, we will go and visit my parents. They are expecting us."

They arrived at his parents' house a little after eight. The house was an enormous, old mansion on Main Street, well maintained with great love and affection. It had a grand porch entrance with a beautifully laid marble floor and a front door big enough to accommodate a bus. In the front garden, two gardeners attended to the brightly coloured flowers lining its edges and, sitting in the centre of its vast lawn, sat a motorised mower. Veronica was both intimidated by its size but also in awe of the beauty that it radiated.

Romulo's parents were delighted to meet her, a docile but very considerate elderly couple. Despite their advancing years, they were still very active and were happy to totter around the house, attending to their sons' every need. They had lived in the house for fifty-two years and the locals always joked that they had more history that the house itself.

His mother was Brazilian by birth but emigrated there at a very young age. She owned a supermarket and a fish market business that bought in a very generous income that supported them comfortably in their twilight years. Her curiosity would challenge any young kitten. She loved to do all the talking and asked many questions. As she barely left the house now, perhaps she was trying to fill the empty spaces left behind by her youth.

She was very uncomplimentary of her son, particularly about his past and had very few positive things to say about him. The mother-son relationship was very strained, mainly because of his bad temper and the fact that he drank far too much. He also had a bad habit of wasting money, giving so much to his needy friends or spending it on unnecessary items.

Veronica was shocked when she told her about the time that he attacked and beat up his ex-wife but, in the same breath, stressing that he wouldn't do that to her because of the love he had for her. She went on to say that she had never seen him act so respectfully in front anyone before, a real novelty for all concerned.

But somehow, that statement offered Veronica no comfort or reassurance. It just reminded her of the visions from her long suffering past. Her words terrified her but, at the age of forty-two, her heart now belonged to him and his to her. He made her feel secure, confident and special and that was enough to commit her life to him.

Romulo's father, on the other hand, was a quiet, reserved, introverted man that had very little interest in the goings on around him. A pigeon sitting on the fence seemed to draw his attention more thoroughly or an aircraft, so high in the sky that you could barely see it. He had nothing to say about himself, nor anything else. Or was it because his wife wouldn't allow him to get a word in edgeways!

During the course of the evening, family and relatives popped in for a flying visit, including Romulo's elder brother and his wife. They didn't stay long, offering just a brief hello and an exchange of a few words. Before leaving, they suggested they meet up soon for a day out, perhaps ice skating at the Lisbon arena, where they'd bring their children along for her to meet.

Veronica wondered if it was a genuine friendly gesture or just plain curiosity as to what the *new girl* was like. She felt like a caged animal at the local zoo, there purely for the public gaze. *Either way,* she thought, *it was nice of them to drop by and appreciated it.*

Over the following few months, Veronica gradually settled in to her new life in Europe. True to her promise, she and Romulo redecorated the apartment, repaired some minor wall damage and invested in some new furniture and ornaments to make it feel more homely. She found herself a new job in town, working in a cafe that was owned by friends of her future husband. It was a temporary, part-time position that carried real risks for her and her long-term future.

She was there on a holiday visa and did not allow her to work and being caught would ultimately result in her immediate deportation. It didn't seem to bother the owners too much, though. Perhaps they knew that the chances of being caught were remote in the extreme and, of course, it was much cheaper labour. Veronica knew she was earning a good fifty percent less than her peers but, at the same time, beggars cannot be choosers. Her working options were basically, zero.

Romulo, despite his constant heavy drinking and rude and crass attitude towards others, managed to hold down his job as a pallet stacker in an electronics warehouse. He had a rolling one month contract as business was inconsistent and he never knew if he would still have a job come the last week of the month. It was a very insecure existence but decent, steady, well-paid jobs were few and far between and difficult to find, even in the restaurant business.

He wasn't a qualified chef, although he could prepare a mean *Bacalhau A Bras,* he didn't want to wait tables and he definitely didn't want to clean the food stained floors. He had previously owned his own establishment and anything else was unthinkable and unacceptable. Returning to the hospitality sector was foremost in his mind but only as a manager; nothing else. Each month he subscribed to *Modern Restaurant Management* magazine just for its job listings, which were plentiful, in the hope of a suitable career.

Its international listings offered superb opportunities but at what cost? Yet another move to an alien country in the pursuit of a stable life. But, in the end, he always had to purchase another issue. More wasted effort, more wasted time scanning the situations of vacant pages and more wasted money making phone calls that always ended in a 'sorry pal, position filled' or 'we require someone with experience in Portugal, not Brazil.'

Any ideas he had of telling his supervisor to 'stuff his job' came to a head in early December, though not in the way that he had planned for. At the worst time of the year in the run up to Christmas, his employers fired him, saying that there wasn't enough work to renew his contract.

It all sounded rather suspicious to Romulo as they were happy to pay him to the end of the month but terminated his contract with immediate effect. He would never had made such an offer to unwanted staff simply because he saw it as bad business. Still, who was he to complain or question?

He kind of knew it was coming at some stage and although he may have hated the job, he desperately needed it. Rent and food payments did not appear using a magic wand and now they were totally reliant on his fiancée's illegal cash in hand job that could, just as easily, go up in smoke. After being told to leave, he calmly removed his bright orange, fluorescent jacket, draped it over the manager's head and, without a word, left the warehouse, holding up his middle finger to anyone that was watching.

He did not tell Veronica what had happened as he did not want to worry her but also planned to go to a job agency that he'd seen advertised a few days earlier in the local newspaper. The agency was close to her place of work on Macala Street, next to the printing factory. He spent an hour there, exploring different options with the desk clerk, who was eager to advise him on this, that and the other. Not that it mattered much, he was just doing what he is paid for in trying to bank finder's fees and monthly employers' contract payments.

As Romulo left the agency, he toyed with the idea of getting a drink at the Men Only strip bar along the high street but Veronica was close to finishing work, so elected to meet her and collect some brownie points at the same time. With the news that he was about to break to her, he needed her as cheerful as possible.

He waited for fifteen minutes outside the cafe, watching the traffic roll past and listening intently to the distant hoots of arriving ships into Lisbon port. The cafe door opened with the ring of a bell and Veronica stepped out behind a departing customer.

"Hello, dear," she greeted. "What are you doing here? This is a first, you are meeting me from work."

He kissed her on the lips and smiled. "Well, this is what I am capable of when I have time on my hands," he explained.

"Sweetheart, it's only 3 o'clock. You don't finish work until five."

Her powers of observation were frightening sometimes. Romulo blamed her mother for it. "Yes, well, something has happened," he reluctantly told her. "Let's sit down here." He pulled a chair that was tidily sitting beneath a table. She sat on the painted metal seat, resting her handbag on her lap. Romulo slumped heavily in to the chair with a sigh.

"What is it?" she asked. "What's wrong?"

"I lost my job today. They told me that there wasn't enough work to justify my contract."

"Oh, no." Her disappointment was clearly evident.

"It's OK though," he continued. "They said they'd pay me until the end of the month."

"That's generous of them." A trace of sarcasm exited her lips. "That's all well and good but what about in two weeks' time? What then?"

He agreed with her point. "Well, I have some—"

Veronica cut him off. "Maybe I can get some extra shifts here," she suggested, pointing her thumb at the cafe. "I'll ask them but I could get in very serious trouble."

He shook his head with disagreement. "They won't give them to you. They're already putting their livelihood in jeopardy." He put his hand on hers. "I have found something else, anyway." He spoke quickly and decisively.

She looked at him in surprise. "What do you mean, something else?"

"Another job," he said, matter of fact. "I've found more work."

"That's brilliant. That's great news." She was clearly delighted. Or was it relieved? Perhaps a mixture of both. "So, what is it, then?"

He held a brief moment of hesitation, as if he were reluctant to reveal it. "A butcher." Even he was struggling to believe what he had just said.

Veronica smiled, which then broke in to a short giggle. "You're joking, right? You're not a butcher, love. By trade, you are a restaurateur. An owner. The CEO. The big boss. You know nothing of the butcher's trade."

"I'm going to be trained," he calmly explained. "An apprenticeship, if you like. I'll be taught everything I need to know until I qualify. Then I will have a skill for life, which means a job for life."

"Well, this *is* a surprise," she commented. "You never fail to surprise me. There is always something up your sleeve." She smiled at her neighbour passing by, making her way to the fruit and veg market. She replied by tapping her on the shoulder. "I think your pie must be extra-large to have so many fingers in it. You are one jack of all trades."

She was clearly very happy with his news and he did have a valid point about the job for life, possibly even setting up his own business one day. The idea was quickly growing on her. "Well done, sweetheart. I'm proud of you," she concluded.

He gently stroked his bottom lip with his index finger. "Thank you, but there is more. It's not here, my love."

She slowly looked up at him, her face changing from happiness to concern. "What do you mean? Is it elsewhere in Portugal?"

The shaking of his head fuelled her concern. "It's not in Portugal at all," he nervously explained.

"Oh, I see." She was beginning to get the picture. "So where are you swanning off to this time? Some dark corner of the planet, somewhere. Iceland, maybe? Or Thailand. Perhaps a tiny little island in the Pacific Ocean with a population of six people and a hundred thousand cockroaches!"

Romulo had dreaded this conversation since the moment he walked from the agency. He expected a cold reception but not this. Her anger and frustration were scary and intimidating. Most people would scream and shout or throw abuse or obscenities. But not Veronica. She knew exactly how to grate his emotions in a cool, calm and collected manner and she knew how much it infuriated him. He wanted to walk away, to do this another day and to give her time to accept but the ball was already charging down the rugged road.

"England," he said, trying to compress the heated exchange. "It's in England."

She sat in silence, her eyes looking into nowhere. It was as if she was trying to process the information, like a computer calculating a complex mathematical equation.

"You're kidding me, right?" she said, after solving the maths problem. "I left my homeland to be with you. I left my family and friends behind. Everything that I worked so hard for. I gave it all up for you. And now you want to take me to yet another new country and restart and rebuild again. I have been here less than a year and invested so much time and money in to our future and you want to just drop it all, just like that. I want to stay here. I don't want to uproot a second time in ten months and for what? You will find another job here, eventually."

"You don't have to come with me straight away. You can stay in Lisbon until I start work and find us a house. Until I get settled in, you can stay here."

"How does this agency thing work? I mean, what do they get out of it? Hang on—" She paused as the pieces began to fall in to place. "Do you have to pay money to the agency, from you salary perhaps? That's it, isn't it? You got to pay them a percentage of your earnings. What is it, a monthly payment? Or weekly even?"

"No, I don't pay anything to them." Romulo sensed an element of victory, giving her an answer that she wasn't expecting. "That's the beauty of it. My employer pays the agency fees," he continued, with the battle nearly won. "I get paid the exact amount that is advertised. The agency also arrange accommodation for me. I'll be staying in a shared house with other Portuguese nationals that also work there. It will be so easy. Everything is arranged for me. All I have to do is turn up."

Feeling that he was on a roll and influencing her choice, he concluded, "And when the time is right, I will find our own home and send for you."

"When will this end?" Veronica asked. She needed more answers and even more convincing. "You have a nasty habit of travelling the world and working before you get bored and decide to move on again. I don't want a life like that. I want a settled and secure life. And if you think it's boring, then fine. A boring life as well. I refuse to keep uprooting just to make you happy. It's as simple as that."

"I'm sorry to do it to you again," he said apologetically. "I understand and accept that. I do, really. But this will be the last time, I promise. We will settle in England and make it our home, even if it's the last thing I ever do."

Veronica aimlessly played with the handle of her handbag as she contemplated his offer. Or suggestion. Or whatever it was. Deep down, she didn't want to leave Portugal. She loved it there. Loved the people around her and their way of life. Loved where she lived. But Romulo was her future husband and her place was by his side.

It was as if he knew exactly when she was thinking. He put his hand under her chin and lifted her head. "We will even get married in England," he said softly. "In one of those quaint little churches in the middle of nowhere. Wouldn't you like that? A traditional English wedding. Doesn't it sound wonderful?"

She took a deep breath. "Alright," she agreed. "But I'm telling you here and now," she continued, pointing her finger directly at him in an attempt to underscore her words. "This will be the last time. I will not move again. I don't care how good or how bad things get. If you start moaning and complaining or you get itchy feet or you are just plain unhappy, then you can up and leave by yourself." She waited for him to take in her words. "I mean it, Romulo and you better believe me."

From his seated position, he gave her a cuddle and a few firms taps on the back. As for Veronica, she had made yet another dubious decision, for better or for worse and a voice from the deepest depths of her mind echoed, 'What the hell are you doing?'

Chapter Eight

It was on May the seventh that Veronica landed at Heathrow airport. She hoped that she was better prepared than when she arrived in Portugal over a year ago. She recalled how inappropriately she had dressed and how cold she felt, even when in a taxi. This time, she wore a wholly jumper, long jeans (not shorts) and a wind sheeter rain coat. But despite her extra layers, she felt so cold, even in the pending arrival of British summer time. She had thought to herself that it might be warmer if she climbed in to a freezer and took up residence there. Portugal was like a lava lake compared to this English climate.

Romulo was made to wait in the arrivals lounge with a friend, their designated driver, for close to eight hours, while Veronica went through immigration control. As a south American passport holder, the officers took her to an interview room, where she was thoroughly questioned and cross-examined. The questions came thick and fast from one official, while the other wrote down her answers on a clipboard. Then came the passport check that seemed to take forever, followed by more questions, particularly about her time in Portugal. Then more breaks, just to wind her up a little more.

She tried to explain that she had someone waiting for her outside and would be going frantic with worry, but her words fell on deaf ears. During her extensive and unwanted detention, they offered nothing to eat, not even a cup of tea and a biscuit. With a whole day lost and a lot of wasted time, they finally stamped her passport, explaining that south Americans were liable for extra scrutiny due to the severe restrictions imposed.

After returning her documents, clip board man chaperoned her to the exit. Did they offer her an apology for the inconvenience? Like hell they did!

As she walked down the corridor, she saw him leaning on a metal guard rail, looking tired. He stood erect when she came into view, exchanging smiles and waves. They hugged each other before he said, "Wow, it's good to see you. I missed you so much."

"Me too." She looked him up and down like a sergeant major inspecting his parading troops. "You need a shave," she observed.

"Yeah," he accepted. "No time this morning. But if I'd known you would take so long getting through, I could have had a shower as well," he smiled.

"Sorry about that," she apologised. "Immigration protocols and crap like that. I can't believe it's taken eight hours. I'm starving. They gave me nothing to eat."

"There's a Costa Coffee over there. We'll grab you something before we leave." Romulo gestured to his companion. "Sweetheart, this is Novak, my friend. We shared a house when I first arrived here. He's going to drive us home."

They traded greetings with a quick handshake.

"That's very kind of you, Novak," she said. "And where exactly is home?"

Romulo had rented a large house with four bedrooms on the outskirts of Bristol, in the west of England. The three spare rooms would be rented out to earn extra income, even if it was against the rules of the contract. One of the rooms as already occupied by a young man from Mozambique named Sergio, a trustworthy, pleasant and friendly chap and a fellow co-worker with Romulo.

Veronica was very uncomfortable with this renting arrangement that he'd installed and unhappy at the thought of sharing their home with strangers that were not part of the family. This was not what she'd envisaged as part of her future. Romulo assured her that it was only temporary, just to bank some extra cash and that they'd have their own home, eventually.

The drive from the airport to Bristol was long and arduous. The M4 motorway was its usual busy self and, together with periodic road works and a nasty accident on the central reservation, the journey extended itself by a further two hours. It was steadily raining, enveloped within thick patches of dense fog. Her first day in the United Kingdom and she could see none of the beautiful countryside she had to offer.

"Welcome to England," Romulo said, looking over to the back seat. "Don't worry, the weather is not always like this. Although it does feel cold an awful lot, even when the sun shines."

On hearing the ongoing conversation, Novak switched the heater on, with Veronica immediately feeling its benefits. "If I have learnt anything about the British people, it would be that they change with the weather. In Spring and Summer they are happy and cheerful and during the Autumn and Winter they are grumpy, moody and miserable."

He smiled at his own personal assessment of an entire nation. "Alright, maybe not all, but a lot. Darling, there are four seasons here and you are likely to suffer the cold with three of them. At least for a while until you acclimatise but, in the meantime, we can fight the chilly air with warm clothing and central heating."

Veronica slumped her head heavily on the seat headrest. "God, I'm hungry," she complained.

After the long drive, they finally arrive in the Bristol suburb of Soundwell. The rain had eased off but the fog continued to make its presence known. Novak carefully parked the car outside their new home, opened the boot of the car and removed Veronica's two cases. Romulo offered him a hot drink before leaving but he respectfully declined, saying that he needed to get home. The two of them watched him pull away until the car was engulfed in the mist and only the sound of a purring engine could be heard.

Romulo inserted his key into the lock and with one quick turn, the door opened. "Welcome home," he cheerfully said. "I would carry you over the threshold but we aren't married yet." He upturned one side of his mouth in a half-hearted smile. "I don't think I've got the strength to do it, anyway. A Tesco bag would be a struggle."

Veronica tightly hugged him before stepping inside, followed by her fiancé and two suitcases. From their next-door neighbour's wall, a black and white cat curiously watched them until the door closed. He then subsequently jumped down and slowly ambled into the fog.

The alarm clock would always go off at 5 o'clock in the morning, without fail, seven days a week, that universally hated ringing sound that bought only bad news; time to crawl out of bed and prepare for work. Every time it screeched out its tunes, he just wanted to throw it across the bedroom against the wall or batter it into tiny pieces with a baseball bat.

Of course, there were decent days to be had at work occasionally but they were as rare as having a lunchtime beer with a dodo bird! It wasn't his fault that he found himself in this situation, blaming it entirely on that *agency* back in Lisbon. They sold him a dream of a skilled, long-term career and, as a qualified butcher, a permanently high salary but working as a packer in a meat factory was a million miles away from their promise.

Instead of serving the local community with expert lamb, pork, venison and beef cuts, he spent ten hours a day wrapping processed meats into cellophane sheets and stacking them haphazardly in cardboard boxes and then spending an hour every evening, in the shower, scrubbing away the foul stench. If it wasn't for his close friend Sergio, sharing a laugh and indulging in long conversation to help suppress the time, he would have quit months ago.

When he told Veronica, she laughed hysterically that opened the door for constant 'piss taking' and endless meat jokes. He remembered telling her that her sense of humour was something not to be desired, which made her giggle even more. All he wanted to do was to return to the hospitality sector and run a restaurant or, better still, own his own. But the competition was fierce and very extensive.

The Bristol suburbs were lined with eateries; restaurants, fast food shops and take away services and, in the town centre, the upmarket and professional establishments including one owned by TV chef Gordon Ramsey, where you pay enormous amounts for a dinner that barely filled the plate. That was Romulo's dream, to own a restaurant that served sports stars, actors, celebrity musicians and politicians and to have the opportunity to mix with Britain's glitterati. But, he figured that it was easier to walk to the moon than to fulfil his lifelong ambition. Still, at least he had a dream and while he had that, he had hope.

Veronica joined him at the meat factory once she had settled in, doing the same repetitive duties. However, she didn't mind doing it. She didn't exactly enjoy it, not many of the employees did, but it was regular work with a reasonable wage packet. Most of the workers were foreign nationals, most of them from the eastern block of Europe while others came from Africa, South America and the far east.

It was a truly diverse place and despite the many different nationalities, Veronica never once heard a single racist comment, jibe or insult. She did question, however, the legality of some of them but quickly swept it under the carpet as it was none of her business. Her documents had been processed a few days earlier, the Home Office issuing her with a Right to Remain visa that allowed her to work and to permanently stay in the country.

Both Romulo and Veronica endured a seven day work routine with ten hours each day, except weekends when it was cut to six hours. They rose from bed together, attended work together and went home together, basically living in each other's pockets, day in and day out. It did, however, make the job more tolerable, but not better, sharing their lunch hour and tea breaks. Everybody needed something to look forward to and, for the time being, this was theirs.

Veronica, though, still had concerns about Romulo's drinking and, with their wedding fast approaching, she asked him to moderate it and just indulge in alcohol at the weekends. He did not like the idea but made a conscious and concerted effort to minimise his habit. It was far from easy, as he knew that he was potentially an alcoholic but would never admit it to anyone, not even his bride to be.

When the weekends did arrive, he would drink like it was unfashionable and would show drastic and worrying changes in his behaviour. After work, he would drink virtually non-stop and would pass out on the sofa watching endless episodes of *Ajuste de Contas* on RTP1. She only tolerated it because it was just one day a week and, as far as she was concerned, during the week, he was dry.

Unlike her marriage to Marcos all those years ago, their wedding was a quiet, small affair in a registry office in June 2002, with just six people in attendance. It was beautifully and elegantly marshalled and conducted and they were happy to share their special day with a gorgeous, warm summer afternoon. The reception, on the other hand, was a noisy and energetic affair with loud music, loads to drink and plenty to eat. The dance hall was packed with friends, professional and personal, all having a lovely time, dancing the evening away.

As she watched the revellers rock and roll, she thought about and wished that her family back in Brazil could be there with her. She missed her daughters terribly and longed to hold them once again but knew it wouldn't happen anytime soon. They had sent her (and Romulo) best wishes and congratulations cards but those material items could never compensate for the real thing. It stirred the sadness inside of her for a short while but didn't let it ruin her special day. As she watched her groom, standing at the bar stacking up the drinks, she thought to herself, *Whatever happened to the small, quaint church in the middle of nowhere*. It would have been nice but she never really believed it.

Romulo departed the bar, carrying yet another gin and, in his other hand, another for his bride. He was buying drinks faster than she could consume them. She watched him as he gingerly staggered towards her, struggling to hold a straight line, desperately trying to stop himself from falling flat on his backside.

He placed both glasses on the table, sliding empty ones to one side to make room. "I got you another drink, darling," he said. As he stood still, he began swaying from side to side. His speech was slurred and partially incoherent, pausing with each word as he tried to summon them.

"Sweetheart, I have a full one there," she said, pointing at the glass sitting beside him, "and I've got another half full one there."

He turned round to look at the table but nearly fell over, using his hand to steady himself. "We are a married couple now." His comment was somewhat random. "We, we g—g—got married today. Are you happy?"

"I'd be happier if you stopped trying to bankrupt the bar."

He was unable to comprehend as he tried to arrange her words in the correct order, his face offering various expressions as he did so. "We've got a- a- lodger, new lodger moving in with us soon—I—I think."

"What?" she said, exasperated. "What are you talking about?" He did not answer as he attempted to pick up his drink. "Darling, leave that alone," she insisted. "What do you mean by another lodger?"

"Hmm, what was that? What did you say? What lodger?"

"You said that we have got another—"

He cut her off by rudely talking over her. "I think- I think." His brain was sinking fast. "I think—I want to throw up!"

She knew that she couldn't get anything out of him in the state he was in. She didn't understand what he was saying and suspected that he didn't know either. She was brought up to believe that drunk people told the truth and his statement wasn't just a pointless collection of jumbled words. There was something sinister in what he said and she didn't like it one little bit. The last thing she wanted to do was to create a scene on their wedding day in front of so many guests. She would have to pick this up again tomorrow, when he was sober and in control of his faculties.

They had no work for the coming week, with both taking annual leave to begin married life together. They had talked about going to Windermere in the lake district for a few days, a mini honeymoon he had labelled it, before the main event later in the year but neither one of the trips was booked. He was either too drunk, too busy or too tired to get it done, just like so many other instances recently. She had offered no complaints and just let it go, but she wasn't about to let last night's comment go.

She sat at the breakfast table eating porridge (as she still felt a morning chill, even during the British summer months) and enjoying her first coffee of the day, waiting for her *husband* to show himself. Sergio had already departed for work and had left the kitchen immaculately clean and tidy as he always did. Romulo had said that he was helpful but he looked after the house as if it was his own and like a second job. He had no family in England and limited friends so he rarely went out and spent his free time cleaning. He also liked to dabble in the garden sometimes, when it wasn't raining.

It was close to midday when Veronica heard the unmistakable squeaks of the stairs as Romulo descended them. He walked into the kitchen, dragging his feet as he did so, his dark hair sticking up untidily, like a punk rocker that had used a full tin of Brylcreem. He was totally naked, like a newborn baby.

"Go and put some clothes on, for god's sake."

He looked down at himself before grabbing a towel from the dirty washing basket and wrapping around his waist. He slumped down into the breakfast table chair opposite his wife. "I feel awful," he commented, smoothing his hair flat with the palm of his hand. "I think I went to town a bit too much last night. Did I embarrass myself?"

Veronica folded up the free local newspaper she'd been reading and tossed it to one side. "I want to know what you meant last night," she asked. "What did you mean by what you said?"

He shook his head and downturned his mouth. "I'm not sure what you are referring to. My mind is a blank after we had our first dance together. I remember that." His mouth changed to an upturn. "Wasn't that romantic," he recalled. "Us dancing to our song, *Chris De Burgh's Lady in Red,* with everyone watching us. Was a wonderful moment." Evasion was one of his annoying traits and she had expected it.

"Yes, it was lovely," she agreed. "But I want to know what you meant when you said 'we will have a new lodger soon'. What are you suggesting?"

"I'll put it on now if you like and we can dance some more." He rose to his feet. "And then we can go back to bed, if you know what I mean." He offered her a couple of suggestive winks.

"Sit down, please," she commanded. "I don't want to dance and I don't want to make love. You couldn't manage it last night and I'm pretty sure you won't manage it now."

He smiled broadly. "Wanna bet?" he said, holding out his hand towards her.
She declined to take it. "Sit down."

"Awww," he said, like a child that had been denied a bag of sweets. "You don't normally turn me down." He leant up clumsily against the back of the chair and, once again, downturned his lips.

"Please sit." Her patience was running thin. Sometimes, he had no sense of priority and, too often, took life as one long joke. "Go on."

With a nod of his head, he sat down, folding his arms on the table. "Am I allowed to make a cup of coffee?"

"In a minute. This won't take long provided to stop behaving like a kid." She sat back in her chair. "Now, tell me. What are you talking about?"

He shrugged his shoulders. "I don't remember saying that."

"Of course, you don't. You were pissed out of your skull—As usual. But you did say it. I heard it loud and clear."

"Hmm, alright." He raised his outspread hand and pointed towards the kettle. "I'd really like some coffee."

"Romulo, please," she shouted. She was close to snapping, like a dried out twig.

"OK, OK. Calm down," he gently requested. "We have two spare rooms in this house and this is an opportunity to earn more money for our future. We will get another two hundred pounds a month, which will go straight in to the bank."

Veronica found him and his argument unconvincing. "No, it won't. It will go to the local off licence or spent in the alcohol aisle of Asda." She knew it to be true but he'd never admit to it. "Who exactly is it that you've invited to stay here?"

He looked away from her, down at the table. "Alfonso." He spoke quietly, almost in a whisper, hoping that she wouldn't hear him and then miraculously decide to forget about it and drop the conversation. But lady luck was not smiling at him today.

"Oh, my god," she complained. "No frigging way. Alfonso is *not* coming to live here. It's not going to happen. I won't allow it."

"It's more money for us, sweetie. It will go a long way to secure our future."

"Romulo, he is unpopular, uncouth and selfish. Nobody talks to him at work nor sits with him at lunchtime. He has no friends because he uses everyone."

Veronica had so many negatives about Alfonso to throw at him that she needed time to gather them. "Nobody likes him because he treats everyone as a servant. He's highly antisocial, he has a foul mouth and he's two-faced. He says bad things behind everyone's back. He can't be trusted and you want to bring him into our home. Even the British workers try to avoid him. George once told me that he caught him trying to break into someone's locker." She violently shook her head. "No way. I don't want him here."

"He is a Portuguese national, experiencing troubled times. He needs my help and I *will* help him. As expats, we all need to look after and look out for each other. We are all a thousand miles from our true home and he has nowhere to turn."

"He is not from Portugal, Romulo," Veronica observed. "His accent is nothing like it. He's conning you. Using you. I bet he only says that just to fit in at work because there is so many working there."

"You have no idea what you are talking about, woman." Romulo felt that this had gone on long enough. He needed to cut it short. "The house contract is in my name and what I say goes. It's my decision and mine alone. He is moving in tomorrow and that's the end of it."

"You're breaking the conditions of the contract. You are not allowed to do this. You'll get us all evicted, for Christ's sake. Don't be so irresponsible." She felt that her powers of persuasion were falling by the wayside. "Don't do this," she continued, shaking her head at the same time. "It will be a massive mistake, believe me." She waited for his response but none was forthcoming. "Have you seen his passport, by any chance?"

"What? What does that have to do with anything?"

"Does he have a Portuguese passport?"

"It's not my business to ask him for his private, personal papers." He wiped the saliva that was gathering on his mouth with the back of his hand. "You, of all people, should give him a chance. Like me, he lived in Brazil for many years and, like me, he has lost some of his Portuguese accent. It couldn't be more simple."

"Where in Brazil did he live then?"

Romulo took a long, deep breath, a sure sign that he was getting bored with the proceedings. "He followed the work all over the country. He is a miner by trade; Coal, silver, whatever was available. So, to answer your question, he lived in many different places."

Veronica suspected that there were illegal workers at the meat factory and she was sure that he fitted in that category. "Honestly, you cannot make this decision without me. I am your wife and we share all the expenses and the running of this house. I live here as well, so it's not just your choice, it's mine as well."

He stood up from his chair, causing its legs to grind along the floor. The towel around his waist came loose, quickly grabbing it before it had time to fall off and retied it.

"That's enough now," he said, raising both hands in the air. "I have listened to the points you've made fairly but the decision is already made. I asked him to move in tomorrow and he agreed. I don't want to hear any more about it." He turned and headed for the door. "I going to have a shower and then we'll go to Syd's cafe for a lunchtime fry up."

Veronica silently watched him as he vanished through the kitchen door until she again heard the sound of the squeaky stairs. She picked up her coffee cup for cleaning and there, sitting on the window seal, she saw the next-door neighbour's black and white cat.

"What does 'finish you off in a blink of an eye' mean?" Veronica asked Trevor, as they kitted up for their day's work.

Trevor placed his transparent plastic hat upon his head and turned to her. "Well, it's an English expression," he explained. "It means to do something quickly and decisively. It usually refers to killing something. An animal, perhaps."

She pondered his explanation for a short while but found herself none the wiser.

"To put it another way," he said, revising his previous, poorly assessed attempt. "It means to kill something quickly with no malice of forethought or, without worrying or even caring about what they'd done."

"Oh right. OK." She duly thanked him for his help before making her way to the meat conveyor.

She had heard this yesterday lunchtime, during an argument between Sergio and Alfonso. Sergio had popped outside for a cigarette and, although he wasn't a smoker, Alfonso had followed him. Veronica was in the loo, washing her hands and the row easily protruded through the open window. What the argument was actually about was unclear as she had caught the tail end of it, but the expression was the final words said.

The dark atmosphere between them was clear for all to see and over recent weeks, they seldom spoke, at home or at work. Sergio had mentioned to Veronica that he thought he was taking drugs in his room of an evening but was by no means positive as there was no concrete evidence to support it. Alfonso kept his room door locked when he was out and closed when he was in. Romulo couldn't care less what he got up to and was quite happy to chat with him in the evenings in front of the TV or to the tunes playing on UK Gold.

She often listened to them while cooking dinner, hoping to discover where he lived in Brazil or where he had travelled. But it was always a lost cause, as he seldom spoke of himself or his past, preferring to listen to Romulo's stories as he eagerly delved into his own past that he had so lovingly enjoyed. Sergio couldn't stand to be around him, staying in his room reading Shakespeare or

Edgar Allen Poe novelettes. He would only come out to clean the house or help Veronica with the cooking.

Alfonso was so uncomplimentary and had nothing positive to say about anyone and it infuriated Veronica when he criticised her cooking. She knew exactly how good her culinary skills were and would spend up to two hours preparing a tasty and healthy meal for them all. The guy was just a nasty piece of work and she just wished that he would get lost but, the future was set, at least for now, decided and enforced by her husband.

There was nothing she could do to change it. What options were there? Leave, walk out, disappear! She was still trying to find her way in a foreign land and she had nowhere and no one to run to. She was caught in a painful bear trap that wouldn't let her go.

Her sister Ines, back in Brazil, yesterday advised her to leave in their weekly phone call, telling her that she should run away and quick. She reminded her that her life was on the same terrifying path as before and was likely to leave her psychologically damaged, possibly unrepairable damage.

Veronica missed her sister enormously, particularly her sensible, level-headed thinking and her suggestion, from her point of view, was probably the correct one. Running away, though, was not the right option. If she was going to leave, then it would have to be a return to her home country. She would need money behind her and a lot of it and there lay the problem. He controlled most of the money, just as he controlled most things in their marriage.

At work the following day, Sergio requested that they all go to a pub when they'd finished, perhaps to the Queens Head on the corner, away from the listening ears of Alfonso. He told them that he had something important to tell them and that he needed to get it off his chest. Taking the aroma of meat with them, they walked in and sat at the table close to the dartboard. If it was in use, then they would have made an alternative choice.

The pub was surprisingly quiet for early evening, with a young couple sitting at the bar and a group of four in the far corner playing cribbage. Sergio purchased the drinks and with them, a food menu was tucked under his arm.

"Anyone for food?" he suggested, after placing the drinks on the beer mats.

"Not for me, thank you, Serg," Veronica replied. "What about you, darling?"

"I wouldn't mind some cheesy chips," he recommended. "Very tasty they are too."

Sergio immediately adjourned back to the bar, ordering two lots. Veronica looked at her husband with inquisitive eyes. "I wonder what this is all about, then?"

He looked over at him, as he handed the bar girl a twenty-pound note. A shrug of his shoulders was his answer. "I know one thing though," he then said. "You smell." A cheeky smile met his lips.

"Lucky the place is empty, otherwise they may have kicked us out."

Sergio returned to the table, tucking his wallet into his hip pocket. "About half an hour, she reckons."

"So Serg," Veronica said. "What's going on?"

"Hmm," he mumbled. "I know I am just a tenant in your home and I appreciate everything you've done for me, but I feel I need to bring this up with you about Alfonso."

"Yes, I figured it was about him," Romulo guessed.

"Just listen to what I have to say please and, if you have to, you can judge me then." Sergio took a swig of his Budweiser and set his glass gently back on the mat. "Alfonso is taking drugs in his room," he blurted. "At first, I wasn't sure. I think he used to lean out of his window and blow the smoke outside but now he has gotten lazy or complacent. Or both. Anyway, my room is next to his and I can sometimes smell it."

He looked at them both as he spoke. "What I am saying is that I grew up in a small village in Mozambique in a religious family. As you both know, my father is the pastor and I really don't want to be a part of any drugs." He went quiet for a second before continuing. "So, if you allow this man to stay in your house, then I'm afraid that I will have to find alternative accommodation after Christmas. I don't want to do that because you two have been so good to me and I love it in your house, but I may be forced to."

Romulo glared at him for a moment, then shook his head. "No way," he disagreed. "I know that we have all struggled to get on with him recently, but you shouldn't make false accusations against him."

"It's the truth, Romulo, I promise you," he assured him. "Haven't you smelt it?"

His reply was immediate and decisive. "Nope, not at all."

"I have." Veronica quickly stepped in to be heard. "I have smelt it, darling. It was just the once, two days ago. I thought it was coming from the students' house opposite but they weren't in as their van wasn't there."

"Are you sure?" He was still unconvinced that Alfonso would do such a stupid thing, especially as a police officer lived just three houses down.

"I'm sure," Sergio said.

"And so am I," Veronica agreed. "He tries to hide it as best as he can. Haven't you wondered why he eats so many extra strong mints? He doesn't at work, does he?"

It was important that she got her point across, into his stubborn head. "We don't want to attract the attention of the neighbours. We are immigrants here, legal yes, but not British passport holders. And you are breaking the rules of our tenancy, as well," she reminded him. "We don't need the eyes of the street on us, and we don't want the copper knocking on our door, either. A quiet, low-profile life is what we need."

"I can understand Sergio saying something, despite the fact that they don't talk, but you have your own agenda, don't you?" His words were harsh, but true. "You have an ulterior motive. You never wanted him here from the start and would take advantage of any opportunity to get him out, isn't that, right?"

"This has nothing to do with how I feel," Veronica insisted. "Listen to your own common sense, if you have any. And listen to Serg. You know, deep down, it's true. Just for once, stop defending him."

Romulo put his glass to his lips and took three large consecutive swallows. He didn't particularly like Budweiser beer as it tasted like cat's piss, but constant nagging ensured it was his only option sometimes.

"Alright, I tell you what I'll do," he promised them. "I'll keep my eyes open and watch him," he explained. "And my nose. If I find out it's true, then I will ask him to leave. How does that sound? Is that fair?"

Sergio agreed straight away but Veronica took a little longer to accept. "One thing is for sure though, the atmosphere in the house has significantly deteriorated since his arrival. And Sergio, the last thing I want you to do is move out."

They decided to make an evening of it at the Queen's Head, enjoying a couple more beers and the cheesy chips, indulging in a game of darts while Romulo challenged a lone lady at pool.

The pub filled up more after 9 o'clock, as the England football team completed their Euro qualifier match against Poland. Come nine thirty, Veronica decided she was hungry after all so, on their way home, stopped at the award-winning fish and chip shop on Gladstone Street. Cod and chips were the order of the day and gorged themselves silly, sitting on the wall of Soundwell swimming pool.

They arrived home close to ten-thirty, greeted lovingly by the cat from next door. The first thing Romulo done was to climb the stairs to Alfonso's room. Music played quietly but the smell was unmistakable, a subtle, faint aroma escaping from beneath his door. One could easily have missed it, it was so faint, but the evidence was clear. At some stage of the evening, he had definitely spiffed and that was all he needed to know. He returned downstairs where Sergio was dropping t-bags into the pot and Veronica, seated on the sofa, was watching the late news on television.

He sat down next to her and kissed her tenderly on the cheek. "Well, sweetheart, you were right," he confessed, pointing his finger at the ceiling. "He is smoking drugs of some sort. It's difficult to notice, but the smell is there, on the landing."

"I knew it," she said, proud that her suspicions were confirmed and that she wasn't just lying. "So, what will you do?"

"Well, he's drugged up now and god knows what else. I'll speak to him tomorrow before he has time to restart. At dinner, I suppose. I don't want to cause a scene at work."

"OK, thank you, darling," she said. "I appreciate it and I'm sure Sergio does too."

"I have to say, I'm not looking forward to it. His behaviour is unpredictable to say the least and he has a short fuse. It's difficult to second guess his reactions or what he might do. Reading him is like—like opening a book that has no words in it." He sighed. "Blank pages for a blank mind."

The following days' work was very awkward for the three of them; well not so much Sergio, as he avoided Alfonso every day anyway, but Romulo and Veronica had to act as though everything was fine. Quick chats and passing comments that they often shared during the day were left in the closet, leaving embarrassing silences with nothing practical to say. Alfonso had asked him if everything was OK, but, pretending he was in a hurry, would rush past him, giving the thumbs up.

They felt enormous relief when the end-of-shift bell rang and now all they had to do was get through the twenty-minute journey home. They just let him do all the talking, complaining about management and how bad his day had been, throwing in excessive profanity for good measure. All they offered back was a 'hmm' or 'yeah' or a 'that's not right.'

As Veronica dished up dinner, a simple, quick meal of Italian Carbonara with a serving of garlic bread, Sergio made himself useful by setting the table. Romulo, reading Good Housekeeping magazine, sat in the living room with Alfonso in silence. Veronica couldn't remember the last time he took an interest in any sort of publication and had never known him to pick up a book. He just wasn't a reader and any reading material they had about the house could fit into a small travel bag. She knew he was trying to avoid any exchanges with Alfonso in any way he could, and she found his chosen method mildly comical.

Sergio helped carry the full plates to the dining table as they all took their seats. They each poured themselves an orange juice, except Alfonso, who pulled out a can of Tenants Special Brew from his jacket pocket, broke the tab with an extensive 'psst,' took a short swig, then set it heavily on the table. Romulo glanced at the unacceptable temptation, thinking how inconsiderate it was of him to bring it to the table but he remembered what Veronica had once said, 'He is selfish and has no thought for anyone else.' Her assessment was becoming more and more accurate than he could possibly have ever imagined.

Once again, they left Alfonso to babble on about stuff that no one in the room was interested in, breaking occasionally to watch action scenes from *True Lies* on the TV. He seemed totally oblivious of the strained atmosphere or maybe he did, but just didn't care. As long as he had his strong lager, a hot meal and a warm room, then everyone else can go fuck themselves. Nothing else mattered.

Veronica tapped him on his leg, the signal to get started. Sergio was still eating but the rest had finished. Alfonso held on tightly to his drink as he watched Jamie Lee Curtis dancing in a hotel room in her underwear. "She is so hot," he remarked. "I could go a few rounds with her." He chuckled at his own sexist comment.

Romulo picked up the television remote, switching it off. He replaced it back on the cabinet beside him. Alfonso looked round, startled. "Hey, we were watching that."

"No, Alfonso, you were watching that," Romulo corrected him. "I need to ask you something, if you don't mind."

He took another swig from the can and placed it on his now empty plate. "Ask away, man."

Romulo nervously licked his dry lips, looking at his glass which he had earlier emptied. Veronica, sensing his apprehension, re-poured him another.

"Are you taking drugs in my house?"

"Now I get the picture," he moaned. "So that's what the silent treatment is all about. I was wondering why the sudden interest in modern day vacuum cleaners?"

"Are you doing drugs in your room?" He knew the answer already but he needed to hear him say it.

"Yeah, sometimes." There was no essence of regret or remorse in his voice. "I occasionally smoke some weed after work. It helps bring me down."

"What about hard drugs? Are you on those as well?"

"Listen, I pay my rent on time every month. I think that entitles me to a little relaxation time, don't you?"

"Not in my house. If you want to relax, then take a spa day," Romulo told him, taking a sip of his juice. "I will not tolerate drug taking around my wife. It's also illegal and we have a policeman on this street. Comprendre?"

Alfonso gave him a long, blank stare. It was as if he was looking into the eyes of a doll, cold, black and lifeless. Romulo felt a cold shiver run down his spine.

"Now you listen, pal." He pointed his finger at him that sat just inches from his face. "You ain't my pal, right? I will do what I want to and not what you expect me to do. Comprendre? Pal."

His heart was thumping in his tightened chest but he had to see this through. "We don't want you here anymore," he said. "I don't want you here anymore. The best thing for us all is that you find yourself alternative accommodation." Romulo wasn't scared of him but every nerve and sinew in his body was tingling.

His laugh was ear piercing, like a lone wolf howling in the night. Sergio watched him carefully as he had seen those harrowing actions before, during their argument. It was a worrying sign.

Alfonso nodded his head, still holding that gruesome smile, exposing his badly maintained teeth. "You are kicking me out?"

"If you want to put it like that, yes."

He stood up sharply, knocking his lager over after banging his knee on the table. "Come on then, big man," came his invitation. His arms were outstretched with his hands waving in his direction. "Come on. What are you waiting for?" Romulo remained in his chair as he witnessed the real Alfonso. He dropped his arms and sat back down. "You are fucking coward."

"This is the real you, aren't it? You pretend to be everyone's friend and then go on the attack at a canter." He adjusted in his chair, resting his elbows on the wooden arms. "None of us can stand to be around you anymore. You bring nothing but depression and sadness into this house and we don't want that anymore."

"I'm not leaving here, no matter what you say," he insisted. "I've nowhere to go and no means of getting to work." He paused before saying, "dream on."

Romulo ignored his attacking onslaught because he had better defensive positions, better training and far better weapons. "From tomorrow, you will have to cook your own meals and supply your own food and I want no more rent from you."

He suddenly found himself remarkably calm and speaking with a clear head. Perhaps it was because he had challenged him to physical violence but quickly backed down. "I will, however, continue to drive you to work until you make other arrangements but expect no other favours. In the meantime, I want you out by the end of January so that gives you five weeks to get yourself organised."

Alfonso remained seated as he gave him a wild glare. "I thought you were my friend, you fuck."

Romulo rose from his chair, followed by the other two and, in solidarity, they casually walked from the living room, leaving Alfonso and his spilt drink at the table.

It was after 1 o'clock when they finally settled down in bed. They had sat awake for a while, discussing the evening's events to the soothing sounds of Classic FM, playing quietly on the digital radio.

Eventually, Veronica's mind gave in to fatigue and fell asleep, cuddling her pillows with both arms. *Peace at last*, he thought, as he watched her. A small clump of her hair annoyingly tickled her nose, causing her to wriggle it. He gently brushed it aside before it caused her to sneeze. Her nose was highly sensitive and she often had sneezing fits, sometimes a dozen in a row. He once joked that he'd make an audio recording of *bless you* so that he didn't have to keep repeating himself.

She looked so beautiful lying in her tranquillity, far away from the harsh world that had rudely joined their marriage. He hoped that she'd sleep through the night undisturbed and let that harsh world torment somebody else for a change.

He, though, did not sleep. He spent much of the night watching the shadows dancing gaily on the ceiling, projected from the old chestnut tree that stood proudly outside their door. He sat at the window for an hour, even though nothing stirred or moved. He watched as the black and white cat briefly appeared, sharpening his claws on the enormous conker tree, before vanishing somewhere in the gloom. Outside was a far cry from the busy, bustling streets of Lisbon, where there was always something happening. It was calming and relaxing and, in its own private way, beautiful.

Sergio had long since fallen asleep, his steady, dulcet tones drifting lazily from across the hallway. It wasn't snoring, just a regular, consistent heavy breathing that was pleasing to the ear.

As he enjoyed Bristol's night time solitude from the window, he heard Alfonso retire to his room, sometime after 3 o'clock. Despite the anger and rage he had shown earlier, it seemed that he was conscious not to make too much noise. He quietly brushed his teeth, muting any potential sounds and softly closing his bedroom door afterwards.

He listened as the lock clicked into place and beyond that, there was silence. It was hard to believe that in this calm, restful atmosphere, there was so much tension and hate. Perhaps, Romulo thought, he might come to his senses and change his behaviour and show more respect and decency. After all, he wasn't always hostile and aggressive, only at certain times, but it was impossible to know when those times would manifest themselves.

Dawn broke over Bristol and the sun began to rise behind the gloomy clouds, revealing a thick frost that was as white as a layer of snow. The temperature had dropped to an eye watering minus eight degrees, converting the colour of the grass. Through the frosted window, it looked like an Olympic size skating rink. Near and far, perched in the trees, the birds began to sing in a musical chorus of tweeting chirps, its joyous tune echoing through the quiet streets.

Romulo watched them with great interest as, one by one, they came to life, shuffling in the trees with fluttering wings. His love for birds had been constant over the years, for what reason he never really understood. Perhaps it started as a young boy, growing up with a small Avery his parents had installed in their back garden. The only book he ever owned and read was the Encyclopaedia of Birds, printed in 1974 and still treasured it to this day.

He recalled happier times as a teenager, fishing in the Rio Tejo with his father in summer and feeding the seagulls with scraps and small fry fish from the net. It was always a spectacle to behold, with the birds diving at high speed and catching their lunch with perfect precision.

He loved to watch the feeding frenzy with a hundred seagulls dancing the tango in mid-air, a concerto of perfect fliers that would impress any red arrows of flight crew. And even more recently, with Veronica at Weston-Super-Mare beach, sitting on the coast wall, throwing handfuls of chips in the air and watching them being caught in full flight, while the slower seagulls scavenged the lose feed on the sand. Wonderful moments, wonderful times. Memories that would remain and out last any high-definition photograph.

Over the next few days, they barely saw him in the house. He kept himself at arm's length and stayed in his room most of the time, not even coming out to make something to eat. They knew that he went to the Kebab shop regularly for his meals but he no longer made use of the kitchen.

Sometimes, after work, he would go straight out to god knows where, without even showering. Perhaps he needed to score some dope or he was terrorising innocent dwellers on the high street. All information about him was now classified and it was difficult to know if that was a good thing or not. They may have fallen out big time but he had been a part of their lives for some time and it wasn't easy to let that go.

At work, they ignored each other, not even exchanging the odd glance. Veronica had asked Trevor, the supervisor, if he could move her to a different workstation, further away from him. He had no problem arranging it as he secretly had a soft spot for her.

He really quite fancied her, in fact and as he subtly watched her moving about the factory floor, eyeing her breasts and bottom, triggering all sorts of sexual fantasies. But she was spoken for, a married woman, therefore out of bounds and he respected that. But it didn't mean that he couldn't make her working time just a little more tolerable. No one would notice, nor mind.

Alfonso wasn't at work that day, he had called in sick with some sort of stomach bug, but Veronica knew it was rubbish. It did, however, give her the chance to speak to Trevor. Now, she could feel a little more comfortable and secure in her job, being on the other side of the building.

The day passed without incident, made easier by Alfonso's absence. After the bell chimed its goodbye tune, Romulo suggested that, instead of cooking, they go out for a meal at the new Greek restaurant that opened on Regent Street. She appreciated his offer but there was chilli con carne leftovers from last night that had to be devoured. She didn't think that next-door's cat would enjoy that too much. Another time she told him, perhaps at the weekend.

They arrived home a little after seven and it was Veronica's turn to be first in the shower. She undressed in the bedroom, put on her thick, warm bathrobe and headed for the bathroom.

The water warmed her cold body, delivering instant heat, as if she were tightly cuddling a radiator. Although she had been in England for seven months, she was still suffering badly with the cold and experiencing her first winter was proving to be a bitter pill to swallow.

With a heavy frost every morning and large ice patches dangerously populating the pavements, three layers of clothing couldn't defend her from the piercing chill. She had never seen snow before, only in the movies and, with the forecasters predicting the first snowfall of the season, she had asked Romulo to change the heating timer to switch it on at midday, so the house was tolerable when arriving from work. He was happy to do it, not just to keep the peace, but also to keep her happy.

She washed herself vigorously all over her long legs, her flat tummy and her firm breasts. In the olden days, she used to wear a shower hat to keep her hair dry, but the stench of meat was happy to reside in her long, black strands. The smell did not discriminate, boy or girl, black or white, rich or poor. It would happily pollute everyone until it was scrubbed away. They used to share a shower together, many moons ago, sensually and erotically washing each other, ultimately resulting in love making up against the bathroom's tiled walls.

Veronica rinsed herself down one last time before turning the shower off. As the sound of the running water faded, it was replaced with muffled voices downstairs. She turned her head slightly, like a dog trying to hone in on an unusual sound frequency. At first, she thought it was the radio or television on high volume but, as the water drained from her ears, she realised it was two different voices, arguing. She quickly climbed from the shower unit, put on her bathrobe and opened the door. Sergio was on the landing, having just exited his room.

"What the hell is going on, Serg?" she asked.

The voices were now crystal clear and they both knew what was happening.

"It's Alfonso," he reluctantly told her. "He's rowing with Romulo."

She looked toward the stairs. "Oh shit," she cursed. "Not again."

Veronica raced down the stairs, closely followed by her lodger. The frantic voices told her that they were in the living room. She rushed inside to see them both shouting, screaming and cursing at each other. "Oy, you two," she yelled. "Hey, what's going on?"

Neither one of them acknowledged her presence, either deliberately ignoring her or too involved in their own petty squabble. Sergio stepped forward and grabbed Romulo around the neck with both hands, pulling him away.

Veronica stepped in front of him, obscuring his vision. "Hey, hey," she shouted, desperately trying to gain his attention. "Hey, what's going on here?"

He leant to one side to get a look at Alfonso. He angrily pointed a finger at him. "He went to view new accommodation today but was immediately denied," he told her. "And then he has the audacity to say it was my fault. You prick." He shoved his wife aside. "You fucking prick," he repeated at the top of his voice.

"This *is* your fault. You are the one that wants me out, so who else is there to blame? This is all your doing."

Romulo took a step back and leant against the wall, breathing heavily. "You need to try again and keep looking." He had very little energy to raise his voice after his exertions.

Alfonso leant his backside against the dinner table, partially sitting on it. He wasn't out of breath and had plenty in the tank for more, but restrained himself, perhaps saving himself for another time. He said nothing but just looked at them with his evil stare.

Veronica took him by the hand. "Come on," she said softly. "That's enough now. Go and have your shower."

He hauled himself off the wall and stood in the doorway. "Like I said, you need to keep looking. You've got until the end of January so you have plenty of time to get your unwanted ass out of my house." He was about to leave the room when he turned around. "Because of your sick behaviour, you will no longer get a lift to work. You can make other arrangements."

"You always take me to work," he reminded him. "There is no other way to get there. No buses go that way."

"I'm sure you'll think of something, a versatile guy like you. Why don't you try walking?"

"It's got to be a two-hour walk just one way." He poked his index finger at him. "You're out of order, doing that."

"If you don't fancy the exercise, get a taxi," he said, offering him an alternative. "I'm sure they would appreciate the business."

"M-o-t-h-e-r-f-u-c-k-e-r," he cursed quietly, but loud enough for him to hear.

"Don't forget now. By the end of January."

Romulo confidently strolled out of the dining room, followed by Veronica and, bringing up the rear, was Sergio.

As the rage festered in his head, Alfonso picked up a coffee cup that sat lonely on the table. He threw it violently at the wall, breaking into a hundred pieces that spread all over the floor, leaving a collection of brown stains on the whitewashed paint.

From the top of the landing, they heard the crashing of crockery from the impact. Without a single word, they each continued to their separate rooms.

With all the commotion and turmoil in their lives, Christmas passed them by virtually unnoticed. Of course, they knew it was coming with the streets extensively decorated with neon lights, constant and repetitive adverts on the TV and everyone at work excitedly talking about it, not to forget the old man in his tatty Santa's outfit, ringing his bell, collecting for charity outside Lloyds Bank. But their own personal celebration never got off the ground.

There was no tree sitting by the window in the living room, glimmering brightly in the nighttime darkness, no decorations hanging proudly from the ceiling and walls, no mistletoe sellotaped to the mirror to steal a snog and no presents beautifully wrapped in motif designed, glittery paper. It was as if it had been cancelled without anyone actually saying it. They hadn't even really discussed it, making no plans and inviting no friends around for a tipple and a bite to eat. It was heartbreaking that it would pass them by without really giving it a second thought.

Veronica loved the festivities, stemming from her time with her family back home, a house that was full of overexcited children and adults, that was a touch inebriated. It was the persistent laughter and expressions of happiness that pulled her heart strings, interacting with the children as they played together, sharing playtime fun with their new toys, watching Christmas cartoons on the television and the utter joy on their faces when dinner was served. As the song quoted, it certainly is the most wonderful time of the year and she longed for it again. How she wished that she could travel back in time to experience it all again. Oh, Dr Emmett Brown, where are you when we need you most!

The new year celebrations, however, had not been disregarded, well not entirely. By default, all the workers had a four-day mini break when the factory completely closed down, whereas at Christmas, they had just Christmas and Boxing Day off. New Year's day had fallen on a Sunday this year as well. So, they had the extra day at home due to the added bank holiday. So, to the joy of them all, no bodies smelling of pork between 30 December and 3 January.

Sergio particularly enjoyed the end of the year and had faithfully watched the London fireworks every year since his arrival in England. He didn't really celebrate Christmas due to his upbringing, even though his father was a pastor back in Africa. His festive celebrations back home were singing a few carols and attending midnight mass at his father's dilapidated church.

The village that he lived in so many years ago had a population of around eighty, living in wooden shacks build on struts. They were partially self-sufficient with a modest size farm that they all worked on with prearranged rota but it only supplied about forty percent of the food needed and relied heavily on charity organisations for donations. Water Aid, though, had installed clean, running water so they no longer needed to scout the Lurio River with heavy plastic containers and water bags.

At the age of sixteen, Sergio was sent to Pemba for his advanced education at the Catholic University of Mozambique and passed six examinations with distinction. The unexpected results opened many new doors for his future and, after working for a computer software company for two years. had the opportunity to work in England.

However, bad luck came calling just seven months after his move, being made redundant from his job due to the loss of four important contracts in quick succession. With the two thousand five hundred pounds of severance money he received, he fulfilled his ambition to take his fiancée Claire and himself to travel Scandinavia, visiting three of its four countries; Denmark, Norway and Sweden.

Eight months were spent backpacking from hotel to motel to camping site and, although the trip drained the majority of the money, they would have that time over again. On their return to the UK and eager to restart work, Romulo recommended him to his boss at the meat packing plant and hadn't looked back since beginning work four days later. Being in a clear minority, he was one of the very few that loved his job and the sound of the singing alarm clock at five in the morning.

Not very long ago, he had heard that the computer company that had sacked him had gone into administration and was on the verge of closure.

Romulo had laughed out loud when he mentioned that they were touring Norway, saying 'Bloody hell, man. It's freezing cold over there. Those countries go into the Arctic Circle. Why don't you go where sensible, sane people travel to, like Australia, the West Indies or the USA'.

Sergio had shrugged it off, as cold climates never concerned him, despite the fact that his origins were from a hot country with just two seasons; the summer and rainy season. He found the ice and snow inspiring and, as an amateur poet, it had contributed to many of his works, such as *God's Beautiful Season*, *Frozen Lake* and *Season Number Four*. None of his writings had ever been published, despite repeated attempts, but he didn't care. Putting pen to paper was reward enough.

He had met Claire in Bristol town centre, four months before his premature sacking, at the bus stop while waiting for the 42a to take him home. She was there every evening at ten past five, like clockwork, standing in the same place, leaning on the window of the Primark department store. Their eyes had met a few times but, being the shy, reserved guy he was, he didn't have the courage to say hello and his culture demanded that he keep clear.

He was black and she, white British and, although it was now generally accepted in the modern world, his lack of experience and interaction sent him constant hesitancy messages. It was a dreary, rainy day that the ice was finally broken, finding her sitting under the bus stop shelter. It was Claire that had begun with her 'queens gambit' opening, offering him a smile and nod.

A conversation ensued which actually resulted in him missing his bus, not that he minded one bit, as he found her company highly addictive and mentally stimulating. She was four years older than him, working as an intern in the Bristol Royal Infirmary hospital, widowed after the loss of her husband to cancer eighteen months ago, with a young son. She lived in Patchway, in north Bristol, on a council property.

Their friendship grew quickly into a whirlwind romance and just five weeks later, they were engaged. A small celebration was arranged, a meal at a Chinese restaurant where both Romulo and Veronica were invited, together with her son and two close friends of Claire. Sergio asked Ravi and Zanab to come, an Indian couple that he'd known since his days as a computer operator. Romulo had suggested that they 'go Dutch' with the bill but Sergio was having none of it. 'No way,' he had said. 'This is mine and Claire's special day and everything is on me.'

Although very much in love, they still lived apart but she often visited him at the house. She would always arrive by taxi and, although she never spoke about her financial situation, he felt that she had no money worries. He figured that perhaps the death of her husband had paid out a generous life insurance. She occasionally spent the night when her lifestyle allowed it, but Sergio always made sure that she steer well clear of Alfonso. It was all with the blessing of Romulo and Veronica, simply because they were all so close and loved him like a long-lost son.

To reciprocate the lovely evening spent at the restaurant, Ravi suggested that they all spend New Year's Eve together at his flat, sharing an Indian buffet, savoury snacks, soft drinks and some alcohol, but as they were dedicated Muslim's, they would not participate in that. He asked Sergio to bring their own alcohol as they never had any and would never buy any either and to ensure that it was a limited amount.

It was a much-appreciated offer but Sergio suggested that they come to Romulo's house instead, as it was much larger than their one-bedroom flat. He also explained that Veronica had already planned a meal and that their invitation was imminent. Happy with that, Ravi's contribution would be to bring a small buffet so that the spread was truly multicultural.

With the short working break now in full swing, they drove to the large Tesco superstore to replenish a few absent food items for tonight's dinner, mainly spices that had run low or run out completely. A dinner wasn't a dinner without those special additives and food was naked without them. Romulo had laughed at his wife's analogy, remarking that only his wife could sexualise a meal. Sergio, who was sitting in the back seat, listening to Arsenal versus Liverpool on his DAB radio, leant forward and tapped Veronica on the shoulder.

"I simply refuse to get out of this car if you don't agree with us to watch the firework on TV tonight," he jokingly said. "I asked you yesterday but you just laughed at me."

"Oh, Sergio," Veronica replied, with that same amused grin on her face. "It's only funny because it's so—English. You'll convert to a Briton before you know it, if it hasn't already happened."

He smirked at her comment. "No way," he reassured her. "I am Mozambican and will be forever and a day. But sometimes you have to embrace the English culture and history. Look at all the important aspects of world history and the United Kingdom is involved in it in some way, in most instances." He paused a moment as he helped Romulo search for a parking space. "Yes," he continues. "African I am, but I love living in this wonderful land."

"Fuck English history," Romulo surprisingly offered. "All I'm interested in right now is parking up."

"So, for the third time of asking. Can we watch the fireworks tonight?" His persistence was comical at not letting it go, like a dog refusing to release a length of rope. They had always admired and enjoyed his dry sense of humour.

"Yes, yes, yessssssssss," Veronica conceded. "You can have the fireworks on."

"Thank you." He sang his acknowledgement, rather than saying it. "Just for that, I'll buy you a big bar of chocolate." He knew that she never ate sweet treats so he would ultimately get to enjoy it himself, unless Romulo stole it off him first.

Veronica smiled. *What a character*, she thought.

The supermarket was very busy, with the customers all there for the same reason. It took over an hour just to purchase eleven items, including the bar of chocolate. On their way back to the car, they saw a big, bald-headed, mountain of a man, covered in tattoos of naked women on his exposed arms and legs. His trolley was filled to the top with alcohol, a large mixture of bottles and cans.

Sergio checked him out before saying, "He is one crazy man. Snow is due on Tuesday and he is wearing shorts and a t-shirt. Still, he's planning one hell of a night by the look of it, so he can't be all bad." He looked at Veronica. "Here, I'll carry those on the back seat." He took the two plastic bags from her hands and she opened the car door for him to climb in.

They arrived home a little after midday, waving to a neighbour as he walked past with his friendly chocolate Labrador. The black and white cat that was lying on their mat, stood up and arched his back before giving way and moving onto the lawn. Veronica couldn't understand why he liked to spend so much time in their garden as she never fed him, just offered the odd bit of attention in passing. The cat watched them until the front door closed, then returned to his warm spot on the mat, briefly licking his paw before settling back down again.

As Veronica filled the kettle in preparation for coffee, Romulo adjourned to the toilet. Sergio asked for a cuppa soup rather than her expertly made espresso, retreating to his room once made.

Romulo walked into the kitchen just as she was pouring the coffee. She passed him the full mug, the one with a blue and white picture of Lisbon on the side. "Thanks, love," he said. "The heating is on. Need to warm up the house before everyone starts arriving." He cautiously sipped the hot drink. "It looks like *he's* not here," he told her.

She looked up. "Alfonso, you mean?"

He nodded his head and said 'yes' at the same time.

Veronica smiled, one that held genuine relief. "Brilliant," she rejoiced. "Hopefully, we can get some peace and enjoy our evening. With any luck, he has already found somewhere else to live and never comes back here."

"Hmm, me too," he agreed. "But with him, nothing is black and white. Sadly, I won't believe it until I see it with my own eyes." He set his cup on the kitchen worktop. "We best start preparing for tonight. There is a lot to do, yet. Sergio will be down shortly to help, he's currently on the phone to Claire."

Veronica removed six beautifully designed dinner plates from the display cabinet, part of a thirty-piece collection, capturing the changing seasons of the British countryside. Each plate, as with all its pieces, represented a different season with stunningly painted scenes and artwork. It had been given to them at their wedding by Pedro, their best man and was considered by them both to be irreplaceable.

Upon seeing it for the first time, it brought tears of joy to her eyes as she admired its mesmeric beauty. She laid them carefully on the already set place mats before continuing with the rest. On completion, the table looked elegantly perfect and would grace any king's banquette. She smiled proudly, with complete satisfaction.

In the kitchen, Romulo was expressing his limited culinary skills by chopping vegetables up into small pieces and segregating them into their own private bowls. It would carry a risk to leave him to do the cooking, as slicing and dicing was as far as he was prepared to go. Better leave it to someone who knows how to do it.

Veronica was just placing the wine glasses in their appropriate positions when Sergio ambled in. He had a look of trepidation and worry.

She stopped and looked up at him. "What's wrong, Serg?" she asked.

"I hope you don't mind but is it OK if I go out tonight instead?" It was never going to be a problem but he didn't want to let her down.

She wasn't expecting that and was caught off guard. "Sure, if you want to," she eventually said. "Where are you going?"

"Claire's parents have asked us to spend the new year with them," he said with sincerity. "And to stay with them for a couple of days. Probably until the

Wednesday. I have to come back by then anyway because, as you already know, we are back at work on Thursday." He lifted his hands in an apologetic gesture. "I'm so sorry. I don't want to let you down, as you have gone to so much trouble. I mean, look at this," he said, pointing at the table. "That is just wonderful, absolutely wonderful."

Veronica quickly walked over to him and cuddled him tightly. "Don't be silly," she told her saddened friend. "Of course, you should go and I'm sure you'll have a great time too." She released him and held each shoulder with her hands. "Claire is your future wife and her parents' home is exactly where you should be."

"Thank you for understanding. I don't know why I have you as such a good friend, but I am thankful I have."

As he turned to leave the room, Veronica said, "And don't worry, I'm sure they will have the fireworks on the telly."

He gave her a full frontal smile, showing off his perfect set of teeth and then darted up the stairs, leaving in his wake a perfect set of squeaks. Minutes later, he shut the front door, to be met by Claire, sitting in a taxi.

As she watched him pass by the window, she smiled and shook her head. *What a silly sausage*, she thought to herself, *but still a wonderful man.*

Veronica concluded her task of placing the wine glasses beside the laid plates and walked into the kitchen. Romulo was still hard at it, cutting up multi-coloured vegetables. "Looks like we are one short now," she explained to him. "Sergio has gone to his future in-laws. He will be there a couple of days."

He stopped chopping and popped a piece of sliced carrot into his mouth. "Oh, right," he replied, munching on the stolen cut. "That's OK. If it's what he wants, then so be it. Claire is a lovely lady and I don't blame him for wanting to spend time with her."

"Are you done here now?"

"Almost, yes. I've just have to prep the broccoli and it's all yours."

She knelt down in front of the oven and peered through the slightly greasy glass door. "The lamb is coming on nicely," she said. "It shouldn't be too long now." She stood up and turned the oven temperature down slightly. "What time is it?"

"Good point," came his retort. "Time to pour a drink and get the celebrations started." He picked up a bottle of sherry from the worktop and twisted the cap off. "Do you want one, babe?"

She watched him as he expertly handled the fortified wine. He would only ever drink Spanish sherry as he had grown up with it through his teenage years.

"Not at the moment, thanks," she declined. "And I don't think you should either, for now. You know what happens once you start, you just keep ongoing. Wait until we eat dinner."

He looked at her, not with malice, but in mild disapproval. "OK, fine," he said, replacing the bottle in its original position. He returned to the chopping board and scooped large handfuls of prepared carrots, dropping them into an empty bowl. He then reached for a floret of broccoli and set it on the board. "Why don't you put some music on and—" He was rudely interrupted by the sound of the front door closing.

Veronica looked at him. "I hope that's Sergio coming back to collect something he has forgotten."

Before Romulo could offer a response, Alfonso strutted in, his thick winter coat stained with what they assumed was alcohol and a cannabis joint tucked behind his ear. He scanned the scene in the kitchen for a moment before looking through the door into the living room.

"Well, this is all very nice, isn't it?" He was clearly drunk but his words were calm and collected. "Expecting visitors, are you?"

"We were hoping that you'd be out all night," Veronica disappointedly said. "But as you have no friends, I guess it shouldn't come as a surprise."

"I have done my new year celebrating early, down the pub." He took a step forward and glared at Romulo, looking him up and down. A small laugh left his lips. "You look like a sissy in that apron, doing women's work," he cruelly taunted him. "I always thought you were a faggot and now there's the proof."

Romulo did not reply as he stood there carefully watching him. He did not accept his gambit as he fought to remain in control.

"You're drunk, Alfonso," Veronica reminded him. "Why don't you go back out or, at least, go to your room and leave us in peace?"

He ignored her irrelevant comment. "Hmm, I'm going to buy you a new year's present. An apron decorated with pretty flowers and an inscription on the front saying 'Faggot Face'." He kept his wild, crazy eyes directly on Romulo as the taunting increased. "What do you think about that then, you queer asshole?"

Romulo's anger, that had sat dormant for so long under his enforced restraint, was fighting to break free and his blood bubbled hot, that could not be cooled by the turn of a knob. The steep cliff beneath his feet was crumbling to dust as he slipped closer to the edge. But still, he did not take the bait that was presented to him.

Alfonso stood silent, awaiting a reaction that never came. As the grinding, relentless voice in his head urged him to change strategy, he picked up the wooden steak tenderiser from the table, twirling it in his hand like a baseball player standing on the field plate, waiting for the pitcher to throw the ball. He casually walked from the kitchen and into the living room, parking himself by the dining table.

They watched him in eerie silence, with confusion and bewilderment. He turned around to face them, before launching the weapon onto her elegantly set table. The heavy utensil crashed onto one of their much beloved plates, sending its broken pieces spinning in the air.

"What about that then, eh?" he yelled at them. "You like that?" As he screamed obscenities and abuse, he continued his onslaught, smashing a second dinner plate, then a dessert bowl. The noise was deafening as wood impacted wood and splintered crockery pierced the air. The *baseball player* caught a wine glass flush in its centre, sending it flying against the wall, broken fragments dancing their way into the kitchen.

"Stop it," Veronica pleaded at the top of her voice. "For Christ's sake, stop."

He could not hear her above the ear piercing racket he was creating, so loud that it scared off the black and white cat that was dozing on the window seal. Veronica continued to beg but the taste of destruction was something to behold.

Romulo, subdued to that point, picked up the knife that lay temptingly on the chopping board. He walked into the living room, squeezing past his wife as he did so. As the indiscriminate destruction ensued, he squared up to Alfonso, holding the knife out at arm's length.

Upon seeing the shiny blade, he stopped his attack, resting his make shift weapon on the table. "Now, there's something I didn't expect," he said, to the sound of cracking debris beneath his training shoes. "A queer boy with a knife." He gestured his head with a nod. "You want to use that on me? You wanna kill me, do you?" He let go of the tenderiser and opened his arms out wide. "Come on then. Let's see what you've got."

Veronica, still standing in the doorway, shaking with terror, looked at her husband. "Darling, please put that down," she said in a remarkably calm manner, despite her obliterated living room. "Don't stoop to his level. You're better than that."

He raised his hand. "Stay where you are."

Alfonso grunted under his breath and eyed them up. "Look at the pair of you," he moaned. "It's pathetic. Living your perfect, little, secure lives in your perfect, little home. Behaving in a way that isn't you. Look at the table, having some people round and presenting yourself like royalty. You're as fake as can be." He scanned the mess that he had harshly designed. "Well, not this time."

"Get out of here before I do something I'll regret," Romulo threatened. "I'm not scared of you, not one little bit. No matter what you do, I'll defend my family and my home to the end, if necessary."

"You have made my life a misery. You want to take away my home and *have* taken away my only means of getting to work. You ignore me like I'm invisible and you add more problems all the time just to antagonise and infuriate me more." He pointed a shaking finger at him. "You'll get your comeuppance, one of these days."

He turned towards the door. "That's not a threat, I promise you. It's a guarantee," he coldly said, as he vanished from view.

"I will not allow you to terrorise and disrespect us in our own home."

"Just remember one thing," he called from the foot of the stairs. "I have no family. No parents and no wife. Nobody will miss or cry for me. I was alone before I met you and I'm still alone now."

The squeaky stairs protested under his weight as he headed for his room.

Veronica rushed quickly but carefully to him, scattering jagged pieces of broken crockery on the plush carpet. They embraced each other tightly, seeking solace and reassurance. It was all deteriorating so rapidly and was already way out of control. She feared for her husband's life with the words he had said and the actions he had committed. He was becoming increasingly violent and aggressive, with body language that a sane person would never manifest. His eyes were permanently dark, glazed and lifeless, as if he were constantly drugged up.

"Darling, we have to put a stop to this right now," she demanded. "He's totally lost it. He wants to kill you, I'm sure of it."

"You're imagining it, sweetheart," came his reassurance that she desperately craved. But it was only partial and was not enough. She didn't feel its sincerity and, she suspected, neither did he. "Look, he is just a sad, lonely man with nothing and no one. Just a bully, passing through our world and bullies only respond to one thing, strength. If we stand our ground and face him when we need to, he will eventually get bored and leave." He felt his explanation was going well. "He's just trying to get a reaction, to provoke me into joining him in his world."

"You need to listen to me," she said. "We should go to the police and report it. They need to be alerted about this. It's becoming far too violent. I mean, look at what he has done here."

She pointed the palm of her hand to the floor. "It can't go on. I won't allow it to go on. I hate being here, in the same house as him. It's like walking on eggshells, hiding and cowering in corners just to avoid him. We could offer him money to go and stay in a bed-and-breakfast until he finds somewhere new to live. We could then change the locks and he'd never be able to get back in."

"No, Nica, no." His stubborn attitude had gotten him into hot water many times before. "This is *my* house," he insisted, pointing at himself. "Mine and not his. I will not be forced or pushed out by him, nor anybody else. I—we have worked hard to build what we have today and I'm not going to allow some pain-in-the-ass cowboy to take it all away. And I'm not going to lose all our savings so that he can live a life of luxury, having everything done for him."

He eased her head on to his chest and groomed her hair with his palm. "Trust me, darling. This is the right and ethical way to deal with it. Like I told him, I will defend you and our house for as long as it takes."

For a long time now, Veronica had asked God for help and guidance and looking for answers in his holy book, but the return messages were not what she was looking for. Like a scratched record, they repeated and reiterated the same reply, telling her to run from that psychopath and to keep on running. But Romulo's misplaced confidence in his own ability to handle it stood firm, like a solid brick wall.

Veronica gently forced herself free from his grip, resigned to that fact that a positive decision was not forthcoming. "We have guests arriving soon," she said. "We should clean this mess up."

It took a good forty minutes to get the living room decent and hoover up the broken glass and crockery. It wasn't how she liked it but it would do as there were still tasks to be done in the kitchen. Earlier, as Romulo rigorously sucked up the shrapnel into the vacuum cleaner, Veronica had removed the lamb from the oven as it was close to burning.

Ravi phoned to cancel and apologise. He had spoken to Sergio, who told him that he wasn't going to be there and they didn't want to impose. Veronica felt there was more to it but she didn't press him. They wished each other a happy new year and said their goodbyes.

"It looks like it's just us two now," she told him. "Ravi and Zanab are not coming."

"Maybe it's for the best," he said, wrapping the wire cord around the cleaner. "I'm not really in the mood for it, anyway."

"Yep, I know." The whole evening ruined by *him* and her prized plate set destroyed. How could he be so callous and uncaring? He would have to be very unstable to behave in such a…

Her thoughts were interrupted by the ringing of the doorbell, its chime cheerfully singing *old lang syne*. *How inappropriate*, she thought, as she opened the door.

To her utter surprise, there, standing on the doorstep, as large as life, was Pedro.

"Oh, my," she beamed. "Pedro." She threw herself into his arms and kissed him all over his cheeks. "My god, it's so good to see you."

"Hello, Veron," he greeted. "How you doing? It's been a long time."

"It has, far too long." She let him go. "Come on in," she invited. "Romulo will be delighted."

She led him into the dining room just as Romulo was putting the vacuum away. "Heyyyyy, Pedro," he said. "This is a pleasant surprise."

They embraced tightly, slapping their hands firmly on each other's backs.

"It's good to see you, my friend."

Romulo gestured to the sofa. "Sit yourself down. I'll get you a drink."

"Not for me, mate," declining his offer. "I'm on the wagon. I see that the wife has got you well trained with the cleaning."

He smiled as he sat beside him.

"I'll get you a coke then," Veronica suggested.

"Thanks, that'll be nice." He slapped Romulo on the leg. "I haven't seen you since the wedding. How is everything?"

He bypassed his question, as he didn't want to lie to his best friend. "Yes, the wedding." His recollection was clear. "I still haven't forgiven you for the best man's speech that you gave. I still hold the embarrassment to this day." The speech wasn't really that bad. He was using it to change the subject.

Pedro took the glass of coke from Veronica's grasp and placed it on the coffee table. She sat down in the armchair opposite.

"So, what are you doing here?" she enquired. "Are you still in London working at the Toyota factory?" It was a happy moment but her smile was just half-hearted, almost forced.

"Yes, still there. I'm in Bristol to catch up with friends."

"You'll stay for dinner, will you?" Romulo asked. "There is plenty there. How much time have you got?"

"Well, I planned to drive back to London this evening but sure, I'm hungry enough to demolish one of Veron's fabulous meals."

"its new year's eve, for god's sake," Romulo pointed out. "Spend it here with us. You can spend the night and be fresh for the drive tomorrow."

"Alright, why not," he easily conceded. He was hoping that the invitation would come his way. He looked at Veronica, her face sometimes showing sadness and tension. "Errr, have I called at the wrong time? I should have phoned first, shouldn't I?"

"No, not at all. You are always welcome here, you know that."

"You look sad, Veron. I can leave if you want."

"No," she answered. "Like Romulo said, we are happy for you to be here."

"What's wrong?" Pedro could feel the heavy atmosphere in the room. "Are you two getting on OK?"

Before Romulo could retort, Veronica quickly stepped in. "It's just that we have a lot of problems with one of the lodgers here."

"Veronica, shut up, will you?" This time, he was ready.

"Rom, I have been your friend, like, forever. You have always told me everything. Tell me the problem, maybe I can help."

"There isn't anything you can do this time." His statement was direct and to the point. "It is for me to solve and nobody else. It's all in hand and under control."

Veronica, overcome by her close friend's presence and the intolerable events in the house, began to cry. She didn't know if they were tears of pain or her way of grabbing Pedro's sympathy and attention and, ultimately, his help. Probably a combination of both. Her sobs increased, releasing the burden of so much stress and pressure over a long period of time.

Romulo gave in to his request. After all, he *was* his lifetime friend and they had shared everything, including a girlfriend once, many years ago. He told him every detail from the beginning; the abuse, the confrontations, the screaming, the threats, the intimidation and even the destruction of the dinner table. He rolled up part of the tablecloth, exposing the numerous dents and gashes in its surface and its excessive damage.

Pedro listened in shock, shaking his head at the more gruesome and upsetting moments. He could not comprehend how this sensible, intelligent, level-headed friend of his could find himself in such a predicament.

He drained the last of his coke but held on to the glass, putting it between his knees. "Veron is right, Rom. You must inform the police and quick or at least get out of this house until it is resolved."

He felt that his advice was sound but, at the same time, also felt that he'd already heard it before. "Listen to your wife and listen for two reasons. Firstly, she is right about this and secondly, she is absolutely terrified of being here. If you don't care about yourself, then think of her."

"Listen, Pedro. I bet you he is up there now, in his room, licking his wounds and thinking of a way to apologise for what he's done." Romulo picked up another can from the table and handed to him. "Veronica seems to forget that she has a man by her side and is not a coward. She is panicking over meaningless words and talk from a guy that knows no other way of treating people."

"Maybe," Veronica said. "But after the things I heard him say to you, especially this evening, it has fuelled my fear and concern. You have let this nutter into our home, against the advice of many people, a man we know very little about, a man that has spent his life moving from one place to another, a man that has a shaded history. Ask yourself one question. Why does he have no friends and family?"

She waited for him to reply but no works escaped his lips. "There must be a reason." She paused as she poignantly remembered something her father used to say. She continued reciting it word for word. "Darling, better a mangy, old dog, alive than a ferocious, fearless lion, dead." She let the words sink in. "The threat is plain and clear for all to see and I prefer to have the old dog in my life."

Romulo slumped back in to the sofa, her final words echoing in every corner of his mind.

Dinner was taken very late in the evening, after 10 o'clock and Veronica complained that it was ruined as it had sat for so long and gone cold. They had discussed everything in depth for a long time, with the occasional adjournment for a bathroom break or to collect more drinks from the fridge. It had been a tense chat with the three of them, pulling it in three different directions. Nothing was really resolved as Romulo still seemed adamant about his beliefs.

The cuckoo clock, that sat on a small cabinet by the dining table, that had survived Alfonso's episode, came to life at the stroke of midnight, it's two tiny doors opening and revealing the wooden bird, cooing playfully as it sang its tune. Romulo always found it an amusing item that bought him joy, but today, it was just another part of a stressful day. He had bought it from a car boot sale a few months earlier and had fallen in love with it straight away.

They each embraced each other, exchanging a 'happy new year' and a 'happy 2003', raising a toast with a glass of Gordon's gin. It should have been a wondrous celebration, but somehow, it just felt like they were going through the motions. *At least Sergio had been spared*, Veronica thought, as he enjoyed the London fireworks in a calm and peaceful, loving atmosphere. She, at least, had the consolation that he was happy in the arms of his fiancée.

She made up a bed for Pedro on the sofa after 2 o'clock, bringing two pillows and a blanket from the airing cupboard on the upstairs landing. But he didn't really sleep, just dozed, like a cat rebuilding his energy in preparation for a day of hunting. It wasn't that the sofa was uncomfortable. Indeed it was, it was the thoughts that dominated his mind. Realistically, he was just an outsider looking in and had not witnessed any of the said events, but he believed his friends. He knew that Romulo was a stubborn bastard as he always trusted in himself and his beliefs but, it often clouded his judgement.

New year's day saw them eventually coming to life close to midday. None of them had got drunk the previous evening, just tipsy. Pedro had to be careful with what he drank as he was fighting to stay dry and because he had to drive back to London. He gave in to Romulo's persistence that he had one drink as the year crossed over into the next but insisted that it will be just one.

As Veronica prepared cereal for their late breakfast with coffee, Romulo sat beside his friend, stacking the pillows on top of the already rolled-up blanket. "What time are you leaving?" he asked him.

"Pretty soon," Pedro replied. "In an hour or so." He looked at Veronica through the door. She was still busy. "Listen, man. I need to ask you something while she's busy," he said. "I don't want her to hear this. Yesterday, you said that Alfonso had been a miner for a while in Brazil, is that right?" He nodded in agreement. "What sort of miner was he?"

"Well, any sort really," he told him. "I don't think he specialised in a specific field. He just followed the work. Where there was work, he would go there."

"OK, well, do you know if he was one of those *placer* miners that work in the northeastern provinces?"

"No, I don't know. I don't have any specifics or details. I really couldn't say."

"You know what a placer miner is, right?"

"I've never heard of it," Romulo declared. "Sounds like some sort of specialist job."

Pedro nodded. "Oh yes, it's a special group alright. Most of them are hardened criminals working for gangsters and cartels and such like. They are all killers. It's in their nature. They shoot people for fun, just to see them fly through the air."

"No way," Romulo doubted. "Where did you hear that?"

"If you talk to the right people, you find this stuff out." Again, he quickly glanced in to the kitchen. "If he was a placer, then you could be in more danger than you realise."

"I don't think so," he stubbornly disagreed. "Like I said, he is just a bully, desperate for people to like and accept him."

Veronica walked in, carrying a tray of breakfast goodies. They cut the conversation short as she was already at her wits' end and did not want to pile more worry onto her shoulders. She set the tray on the coffee table and sat her favourite armchair. They all helped themselves to the cereal, corn flakes flooded in milk.

"Have you noticed that *he* hasn't come out of his room at all, not even to go to the bathroom?" she observed.

"There you are," Romulo said. "Too damn scared to show his face."

"Don't you think it's a little strange?"

"A coward will always be a coward. Anyway, he *has* come out, when we are not at home or when we are sleeping," Romulo told her. "Haven't you noticed that he's been helping himself to our food, even though he no longer pays us anything?"

"Well, for an unstable man that seems to have no fear, I find it strange." She took a sip of her sugared black coffee. "What the hell can he be doing up there?" In her tormented imagination, it felt like a black mamba snake preparing and patiently waiting to strike. It made her shiver.

After completing breakfast and a quick shower, Pedro prepared for his departure. They walked him to his car, an immaculate red Toyota, possibly bought at a reduced price by his employers. Veronica kissed him goodbye before hugging his very good friend. "Remember what I told you and please, bear it in mind," he whispered in Romulo's ear.

He nodded. "Drive carefully and have a safe journey back."

Pedro gave them the thumbs up and a smile. "Love you both," he sincerely said.

He climbed into the driver's seat, closing the door behind him. Romulo tapped on the window. "And don't be a stranger for so long next time," he demanded.

"I'll see you soon," he promised.

He inserted the ignition key into the lock. Planet Rock blared loudly from the radio, playing *Lovedrive* by the *Scorpions*. He gave them one last look, accompanied with a smile and then slammed his pride and joy into first gear. Veronica waved as he sped off down the road, soon to disappear beyond the bend.

From the top window of next door, the black and white cat watched intently at the goings on outside, before settling back down into its comfortable warm spot.

And, from the top window of their house, through the drawn curtains, Alfonso stared blankly at them, unmoved, as they walked back into the house. He closed the gap in the curtain, shielding the room from daylight.

Using a straw, he snorted two lines of cocaine deep into his nostrils and sat on the bed as his brain began to numb. From the top drawer of his small cabinet, he removed the kitchen knife that had lain dormant for a couple days. He spat on the sharpening stone, spreading the saliva evenly with his thump and began to gently run the twelve inch blade along its abrasive edges.

Chapter Nine

As their mini new year break had come to an end and work beckoned tomorrow, they choose to have an early night. It wasn't unusual for them to sleep by 10 o'clock as they were such early risers, but locking themselves in their bedroom and visiting dreamland gave them much appreciated relief.

He had noticed that Veronica was sleeping a little better recently but not faring so well during the day. She constantly put on a brave face but she couldn't hide her body expressions and demeanour as she wasn't a natural liar or actor. He so desperately wanted to shield and defend her from the relentless pain and suffering. Everyone was against his decisions, even his long faithful friend, but he had to do what he thought was right. After all, he was the man of the house and had been taught by his parents to always stand up for what was right, whether his choices were debatable or not.

After brushing his teeth, Romulo opened the bedroom door to a mild grinding of its hinges. Some weeks ago, he had bought a can of WD40 to oil them, but had not got round to using it. Somehow, there always seemed to be other things to worry about.

Veronica was sitting on the bed, undressing. He loved to watch her as she removed her clothing. She seemed to take an age in doing it, as if she were deliberately teasing and tantalising him and once, a long time ago, it would result in making love. But, as with so many things in their lives, sex was no longer a priority. He couldn't remember the last time they shared an intimate night together, having to accept that a midnight cuddle was the closest that they'd gotten to any eroticism.

He watched as she expertly unclipped her bra, her long dark hair falling from her shoulders into place, draped down her back. She still looked beautiful and gorgeous and could make any lady half her age appear ordinary.

Romulo sat on the left side of the bed, where he always slept and placed his hand on her thigh, stroking it softly. It was not a sexual invitation, but rather a touch of reassurance. "It'll all be over one day soon," he said. "And we'll have our lives back."

She placed her hand on top of his, a touch of acceptance or perhaps in an effort to stop him from stimulating her sensitive erogenous zone. "I hope so, sweetheart," she prayed. "My constant headaches just won't go away." She looked down at a partially obscured object laying on the bed. "What's that?" He hesitated before picking the object up into full view. She was surprised at what he held. "What the hell is that for?"

He briefly looked at the knife before secreting under his pillow. "It's a precaution, that's all," he explained. "The door is locked so he can't get in but with it here, it might give you some peace of mind." He pressed on the pillow firmly, like a teenage boy hiding a girlie magazine from his parents. "Maybe you are right, OK," he said, beginning to doubt his course of actions. "Yes, maybe he is dangerous and maybe I have underestimated him. I just don't know, but I thought it a wise decision to have it with us."

She was surprised at his change of heart and appreciated his choice. Feeling more secure would help their rest come easier and he had been right as well. The extra protection, like an injected shot of solitude and calm in the arm, saw them both drift off quickly, into a deep sleep.

Two rooms away, on the far side of the landing, Alfonso poked and stabbed the tip of the now sharpened knife into the bedclothes, leaving a number of small holes in the duvet.

The alarm yelled out its brash tune, cutting short and rudely interrupting their almost perfect slumber. It had been their best night's sleep for some time and they didn't appreciate its premature conclusion by a complaining digital clock. Its blue LED lights read 04.45 AM and underneath, in a slightly darker shade, it said 03 Jan 2003. Time to get up and return to work.

Romulo rolled over and switched it off. On work days, he always arose before his wife, allowing her to steal a little more sleep as he prepared breakfast, the lunchtime sandwiches and the thermos. He climbed out of bed, slipped into his warm slippers and began his day.

Her extra nap was suddenly ended by a distant screeching sound that seemed to find its way into her dream or was it part of it? Intuition told her otherwise, as she tried to assess what it was. She walked to the window, pulling the curtain apart and peered outside. Frost was forming around its edges and a dusting of snow had fallen at some stage, with a light covering, but nothing stirred and nothing moved, not even the cat. She expected to see some sort of commotion outside but the silence dominated the darkened sky.

She walked to the bedroom door, picking up a rogue sock from the floor and tossing it on the bed. As she opened it, there she saw Sergio standing in the hallway, leaning on the banister. "Morning, Serg," she greeted. "I thought you were staying at Claire's and going straight to work from there."

He did not give her an explanation. "Did you hear that noise?" is what he offered.

She nodded. "Yes, I did. I thought was it an accident or something," she assumed. "It sounded like a car slamming on its brakes. There is snow on the ground."

"I think it came from inside the house."

Veronica felt a shiver run down her spine. "Are you sure?"

He slowly nodded his head a few times. He was convinced.

She took a few steps and stood on the top stair. "Romulo," she called out. The only reply was the light howling of the wind outside. "Romulo." Her shout was louder but still nothing. She began to question the silence, something that she had yearned for so long. "Stay here," she told Sergio.

"No," he quickly replied. "Let me go."

"It's OK," she insisted, holding up her hand. "Just wait here."

As she turned to descend the staircase, she froze, as her eyes struggled to focus in the darkness. Something didn't look right on the bottom landing, as if the furniture had been rearranged or a piece added. "Turn the light on, Serg," she asked him.

The flick of the switch revealed the figure of Alfonso standing there, his hand resting on the banister post and one foot on the bottom step. She did not notice the knife in his hand until the blade caught the light.

Veronica stood there, unable to move, as her brain processed the data. The fear and terror began to rise as it became apparent. "Oh, god," she mumbled quietly. "Oh, no. No-no-no-no," she repeated as the panic set in, her voice increasing to a piercing shout. She held on tightly to the banister rail as her fear become a reality. "Romulo," she screamed, her voice echoing through the house.

He slowly began to climb the stairs, in an almost deliberate manner, never taking his eyes off of her. As he gained height. Sergio stepped into view from behind her, in a show of strength and support. Alfonso stopped midway, raising the knife at arm's length. "Well, well," he coldly said. "So you're here as well."

Under a steady stream of tears, Veronica began to walk down but he held his position, not allowing her to pass. "Get out of my way, you sick fuck," she yelled. "I want to see my husband." She moved against the wall, trying to squeeze past, but she moved with her. "Let me pass, Let me pass."

He waved the knife in front of her, the blade inches from her face. "Up you go," he commanded. "You don't need to go any further."

Her heart thumped in her chest as the blade drew nearer. Its super sharp point caught her on the chin, drawing a thin line of blood, the injury stinging harshly but she felt no pain. She began to back up the stairs, unable to divert her eyes. Her crying sobs persisted but somehow managed to remain calm. After all, it was still unclear what had happened downstairs. "Please," she pleaded. "Please. Let me go to my husband."

"Keep going," he said, still waving the knife.

As she reached the top step, Sergio took her arm, guiding her into the hallway. They continued to back up as he slowly moved forward.

"Both of you, in there," he said, pointing the knife at her opened bedroom door.

"Romulo," she screamed again at the top of her voice. "Please, help us." His silence ripped through her heart and tapped into her fears. "I'm going to my husband." Her terror had been overrun by her desperate need of the truth. "Get out of my way."

As she tried to shove past, he raised his hands and violently pushed her towards the door. As she stumbled backwards, she collided into Sergio and they both fell into the room. He stood by them as they lay on the floor.

"Like I said, you don't need to go down there," he growled. An evil, unstable grin appeared on his lips. "There's nothing he can do for you now."

As Sergio tried to climb off her and get to his feet, Alfonso launched a kick with such force that it sent him rolling back, catching him directly on the cheek, to the dull sound of cracking bone. He then picked Veronica up by her pyjamas, tearing the top on the arm and popping buttons off, dragging her further into the room. As he stood there, they both sat up, leaning against the bed.

It was then that she noticed her injury, the thumb webbing on her left hand had been sliced, leaving a deep gash that was bleeding heavily. She gingerly hauled herself up in an attempt to sit on the bed, wincing at the excruciating pain that drove through her hand. She reached for the rogue sock that lay on the bed and carefully, but tightly, wrapped it around her thumb, securing it with a black hair band she pulled from her hair. Sergio sat on the carpet, holding his cheek, dazed and semi-conscious, as the pain ripped through his skull.

Veronica looked into his black, soulless eyes. He stood still and motionless, like a statue on display in a waxworks museum. "Is my husband dead?"

Being denied the right to attend to him, the necessity to ask was her only way forward and now, trapped in her room with this knife wielding manic, she needed *him* to divulge the truth.

He stepped forward, crouched down on his heels and stared menacingly at her. "Well, with a number of holes in his chest, I think that's a distinct possibility, don't you?"

She looked down as the tears flowed freely, crying uncontrollably. "Why?" she said quietly and then screamed it out loud, "Why?"

"Your husband's dead," he repeated, as if trying to drill it into her. "He got what he deserved and now you're going to watch your black friend die as well."

Veronica jumped from the bed and lunged at him. She could not allow the indiscriminate, callous murder of a man that bought only happiness and cheer into the house; a soft, gentle and lovely man that had done nothing to harm him.

"No," she demanded. "No more. Leave him alone, for god's sake."

He fought back and won out easily. He was bigger, stronger and faster and their body strengths were incomparable. He swung his arm, hitting her on the side of the face, knocking her backwards, falling over the corner of the bed, to the floor. A loud ringing sensation sounded in her ear as a thin trickle of blood snaked its way down her cheek. Partly stunned, she rolled over and sheepishly climbed to her feet, steadying herself on the bed.

She looked at him as he grabbed the collar of Sergio's bathrobe, dragging him flat to the floor and sitting on his stomach. He picked up the knife and, without any hesitation or sense of regret, thrust it powerfully into the side of his neck. The blade easily penetrated his skin and then, with a much gentler push, slid it further in until it protruded out of the other side.

Veronica opened her mouth to scream but nothing came out and she could form no words on her lips. She watched in terror as he yanked the knife out, causing blood to intermittently spurt from both wounds, spraying frenetically in every direction. Sergio tried to cover the injuries with his hands but his restrained arms were imprisoned by Alfonso's legs. He kicked out frantically as his strength began to desert him and his brain began to fog.

As his own blood tunnelled into his lungs, he began to choke as his airways became blocked, causing him to gurgle in spasms. With the rejection of the red tissue by his lungs, he coughed and spluttered, ejecting spots of blood from his mouth and nose.

Transfixed, as if drawn to the violence by some unseen force, Veronica stood there, unable to move. Her senses recorded and implanted every detail into her memory, ensuring that replays were available over and over whenever it had the inclination.

As her brain began to accept what was unfolding before her eyes, common sense kicked in, shouting and screaming at her to run, commanding her to run, run and keep on running. She stepped from the bedroom and, with a complete lack of care and attention and in total panic, she charged down the stairs. She halted at the bottom and hesitantly looked along the hallway, into the kitchen.

Romulo's legs lay in the doorway, lifeless with no sign of movement or motion, his pyjama trousers soaked with blood from the small puddle that has accumulated beside him. She stared at the devastating image for a few seconds, now with the realisation that her husband must be dead.

Alfonso intently watched the life force drain from Sergio, as if it held some sick, significant fascination. His legs and body ceased to respond, his open eyes blankly looking up into nowhere, his mouth agape, as if in protest, forever frozen in time. He looked at the blade with its smudged streaks of blood, studying the gory red patterns, before forcing it into him again. And again. And again. It ripped into the side of his stomach, leaving large gaping wounds, but bought no reactions, no screams of terror or pain and no defensive challenges.

Downstairs, in a flood of tears and in induced pain, Veronica called his name for the final time and, to the sounds of silence, she wildly opened the front door, crashing it into the hat stand that stood behind it, its hanging arm breaking through the window.

ith all the strength she could muster, she raced blindly into the early morning darkness and the freezing winter air. In her pyjamas and nothing on her feet, she charged along the deserted street, yelling for help at the top of her voice with shrieking cries, but nothing stirred. No lights came on from the passing houses, no curtains were drawn and no front doors opened. Her screams fell onto a sleeping neighbourhood or on to those that were too scared to come to her assistance.

Upon hearing the commotion outside, he rushed out after her, trying to get a fix on where she had gone, but in the cold, heavy atmosphere, her screams echoed and bounced erratically through the rows of quiet houses. The yelling voice was unmistakable but seemed to emanate from different directions. He turned his head to one side and then the other, trying to pinpoint her exact location.

Veronica had seen him moving quickly along, on the other side of the road. For some reason, her feet hurt badly and knew she would be unable to outrun him. In a state of panic, she crawled beneath a car, positioning herself in its centre, the tarmac freezing and then sticking to her skin. Her warm breath gently cascaded from her mouth, quickly evaporating into thin air. From underneath the car, she looked for his movement but the many parked car obscured her vision, aided by the darkness. All she could see was the black and white cat, gracefully strutting homeward bound.

And then, standing on the corner of Adelaide Hill, she saw him, his winter steel toe capped boots, twisting and turning in the thin snow, as he looked around for her. She shuffled back towards the pavement to further shield herself from discovery, watching closely and waiting nervously for his next move.

He stood there quietly, like a tiger lying in wait for its prey. Quiet mumblings of fear escaped from her lips as she stared but he remained motionless. What was just seconds felt like hours with his terrifying presence stretching out in time. And then, finally, he took a few steps forward before stopping again in the corner.

He listened vehemently but could only hear the distant hum of traffic, racing along the Ring Road a half a mile away. Unable to pinpoint her position, he turned left and sped along Adelaide Hill. If he had remained calm and not been guided by his deep desperation to catch her and commit murder number three, he could have followed her faint foot prints that had embedded themselves in the thin layer of snow.

Veronica exploded with delight and relief as she watched him disappear along the side road, moving away from her makeshift hideaway. She dragged herself to the edge of the pavement and crawled out from beneath the car, scrapping her spine along its seal. Her body was dangerously cold and the scrapping impact injected significant pain along her back, but she didn't care. The chance to escape that maniac had presented itself and she just wanted to get away.

She slowly climbed to her feet, her heavy breathing consistent and her body badly aching all over. She started to run again, almost permanently looking behind her to see if she was being pursued, as if she were running backwards. The soles of her bare feet began to sting with pain as she ran, stepping heavily on loose stones and sharp debris. The intolerable, freezing cold air continued to quickly numb her unprotected body, but her escape was a priority.

Just ahead, on the main road in the distance, she saw a car passing by, moving slowly in the treacherous, icy conditions. She raised her arms and waved insanely, like someone signalling a passing helicopter, calling and screaming for it to stop. But it didn't, as it vanished from view and continued on its journey. She kept on running, urged on eagerly by her survival instincts, desperate to reach the possible sanctity of the normally busy Soundwell Road.

As she approached the main junction, to her total relief, she saw someone sitting under the shelter of the bus stop, adjacent to the Leisure Centre. As if her body had had a shot of adrenaline, she found renewed strength and ran quickly towards the awaiting passenger, shouting loudly with her hands in the air. As she drew nearer, the image became clearer. It was a young woman, dressed in warm multi-layers with a bobble hat and a scarf around her neck. She ecstatically ran across the main road, without checking for approaching traffic and called out to her.

"Help me," she screamed. "Please, help me. Someone is trying to kill me." She reached the bus stop and leant against it, gasping for breath. "Help me," she pleaded. "I'm in danger. He has already killed two people." Her voice was shaky and partially incoherent, speaking fast in an attempt to get her message across quickly.

The lady appeared hesitant at first and trepidatious, fused together with confusion and apprehension. She stood up and backed away slightly as Veronica continued with her verbal, mixed up mumbling. She looked her up and down, noticing the bleeding on her hand and the injuries to her feet. The belief in her genuineness grew as she saw how she was dressed. This poor lady was in need of immediate help.

"Calm down," came her offer of reassurance. "Slow down and calm down. You should sit."

Veronica turned around and looked along the street she had just exited. There was no sign of the manic with the knife. "Please," she said. "Do you have a mobile phone?" she quickly asked. "Call the police please, for god's sake."

As the young lady fished through her bag, Veronica turned again to recheck. It was then that she saw two headlights appear on the road, at the top of the hill, in the near distance. As the vehicle closed in and became clearer, it was as if heaven sent, for the vehicle was a police car.

Veronica rushed into the road, jumping up and down, aggravating the numerous cuts on her feet, her arms high in the air, begging for them to stop. The car slowed down as she came into view, halting a few yards away.

An officer climbed from the passenger seat and walked tentatively towards her, placing his cap on his head. "Are you OK, madam?" he politely asked. "Is everything alright?"

She ran to him and threw her arms around him. "Oh, thank god," she said, with enormous relief in the voice. The policeman was like a knight in shining armour, there to save and defend her. "There's a man chasing me with a knife," she explained, still talking fast and with little control. "My husband is hurt," she continued. "He's been stabbed by him. I think he's seriously injured. Please call an ambulance."

"Calm down, madam and speak slowly. You are talking too fast." He looked round at the police car in the centre of the road, its engine ticking over, pumping out fumes that quickly evaporated in the cold air. "Come on," he said, taking her by the arm and guiding her to the vehicle. "Let's sit in the car and you can tell me all about."

Veronica thanked the bystander at the bus stop for her help, who just stood there speechless and bewildered. She climbed into the car, assisted by the officer, who placed his hand on her head, closing the door behind her. He sat down next to her.

"OK, tell us what's happened," he requested. "And stay calm and talk slowly.

"There's a man after me. He has a knife. I think he stabbed my husband. He didn't respond when I called him." It was very difficult for her to recall the details as the painful images flashed through her mind. Again, she began to cry, taking deep breaths to summon up some control. "And my friend upstairs," she continued. "He's dead. Oh, god, he killed him. You need to call an ambulance."

He looked at the driver. "Reg," he said. "Get two ambulances here and some backup. Tell them to dispatch every officer they can. We may have a murderer wandering freely on the streets." He turned to Veronica. "What's the address, love?"

As she gave him the details, the police car pulled away, moving for a couple of minutes, before parking up. "Madam, go through that white door and wait in there," he insisted, pointing his finger. "It's the police station. You'll be safe there. And stay there, OK. Do not go outside for any reason."

She was met and assisted by a WPC who helped her inside. From the front desk, she heard the siren blare out loudly and saw the flashing lights bouncing along the white painted brick wall. Seconds later, it was gone and the siren gradually vanished out of earshot.

The WPC, who had introduced herself as Alicia Ascott, led her to an interview room, where she was told to remove her pyjamas and given a white police issue jumpsuit to wear, until alternative clothing could be provided. She was told that her clothing was required for the investigation and possibly needed for evidence. Her night clothes were placed in a large plastic evidence bag and taken away by the on duty constable.

WPC Ascott assisted Veronica to sit down and she sat at the table next to her. She gently took her hand. "How are you feeling?" she asked with genuine concern on her face and in her voice.

With the euphoria of finally escaping her terror ordeal, she could only cry. She covered her face with her hands as the powerful feelings of relief and the pain and horror of witnessing her friend murdered began to kick in. Her cries and sobs became more prominent as her tears dripped from her wrists on to the table, creating an ever enlarging puddle.

"I'm so sorry for what you have been through, Veronica," she sympathised. She removed a handkerchief from her uniform pocket and placed it in her hand. "The ambulance will be here soon to take you to the hospital."

She looked up, gently dabbing her damp cheeks. "I'm fine," she insisted. "My husband is the one that needs it. Get one to him quickly."

"Keep calm," WPC Ascott said quickly, using her professional training to keep any panic attacks in check. "There is already one on the scene. It's all in hand. But you need to go as well. You have a nasty injury on your hand, your feet are also badly injured and your body is covered extensively in cuts and bruises."

"I saw Serg murdered, right in front of my eyes. I watched as he cut his throat." Her tears continued to flow as the images began to materialise in her mind. "Oh, my god. I let him die and I did nothing to help. I just—just—watched," she paused as she tried to compose herself. "My husband, he didn't answer me when I called him. He must be seriously hurt." She looked up at the WPC. "Is he alright? Have you heard anything?"

"The investigation is ongoing, Veronica. When we hear anything, we will tell you," she promised. "At the moment, our priority is to get you checked up."

A quiet knock sounded on the door and then opened and the on duty constable poked his head round. "Excuse me, ma'am," he apologised. "The ambulance is here."

She nodded as the constable pushed the door fully open. WPC Ascott put her arm around her waist and held Veronica's arm with the other, assisting and guiding her from the room. Just outside the door, two paramedics stood in waiting, together with a wheelchair.

At the hospital, Veronica was duly medicated before fourteen stitches were put in her hand. After a thorough inspection of her feet and a precautionary x-ray, two small pieces of glass were found in the ball of her left foot and immediately extracted. The doctor also explained that they were mildly frost bitten, but they would be fine by keeping them warm. 'Wear socks for the next few days and the uncomfortable sensation will gradually vanish,' the doctor had said.

It was close to midday that Veronica was eventually signed off and discharged into the care of a waiting police officer and subsequently driven back to the station. She was taken to the staff room and met by two female police psychologists, wearing name badges, identifying them as Lisa and Amy. With a smile from Amy, she was gestured to lay on the plush, leather sofa, an invitation Veronica greatly appreciated. She was physically and mentally exhausted, as well as in shock, traumatised and in severe pain.

Amy sat on the edge of the sofa, resting her arm on its back. "Veronica, I know you are very tired, but a doctor is coming to visit you sometime today," she said. Her voice was gentle and relaxing, almost hypnotic and the soft whispering tones filled her with reassurance and security.

"Also, we can tell you that he has been caught. He is being held in a police station in the town centre." She moved her hand from the sofa and laid it on her arm. "So, you do not need to worry about where he is, OK. He is safely locked away. He is not going to hurt you anymore." She looked up at her colleague. "Lisa and I are here to look after you, to help and guide you for as long as you need us." She softly tapped her hand on her arm a couple of times. "So, what I'd like you to do is rest for now. Sleep would be advisable, if you can. We'll wake you up when the doctor arrives."

Lisa picked up a blanket that sat solo on a table chair, shook it free and laid it over her, adjusting the top so it lay up to her neck.

"Thank you," Veronica said, before looking back at Amy. "What about my husband?" she desperately enquired again. "Is he OK?"

"I'm sorry, Veronica, but I have no information right now," she apologetically explained. "Most important is that you rest. All of your questions and I know you have many, will be answered, but for now, one slow step at a time."

Lisa took a step forward. "When you wake up, we will arrange something hot to eat for you and a drink. You've been through a horrific ordeal and your body is crying out for rest. It needs to shield and defend itself from its exhaustion and the psychological terrors, stresses and pains it is enduring." She bent down and straightened the edge of the blanket. "In simple terms, Veronica, your body needs to shut down, at least for a while."

"An officer will be sitting outside the door, just in case you need anything," Amy told her. "Rest now. You are perfectly safe and nothing is going to happen to you."

They both departed, closing the door behind them. Veronica closed her eyes, and although her body insisted that she sleep, it would not come. The terrifying images entered and re-entered her mind, over and over, time and again at Sergio's body being cut to pieces. Veronica's very being, in conflict as her body craved sleep, as her mind reran the horror scenes and as her heart wept for her husband, all fighting for the possession of her soul.

Predictably, though, it was her body that won out on the battle, as her heart and mind raised the white flag of surrender to the advancing army of fatigue. Her heart closed, her mind shut down and she fell into a deep and heavy sleep.

It was a warm, beautiful, sunny day, as day trippers and holidaymakers alike shared the sandy beaches of St Ives in Cornwall. Children ran in the surf, their parents looking on as they laughed and played, while others built sand castles using buckets that had been purchased from the tourist shop. Scores of adults lay on lilos and beach towels in the beaming sun, hoping to steal a genuine but rare English suntan.

The queue was extensive as Mr Whippy dished out ice cream cones and ice lollies to those that were overheating. Further out beyond the boisterous children, a hundred sea surfers lined up to mount their surfboards, like a gathering of sheep in a valley, to showcase their balancing skills, all attired in the same coloured wet suits, preparing for the amateur competition. Occasionally, a dog sped past, chasing a stick or ball that had been thrown into the sea by their owners.

She sat on a blanket they'd *borrowed* from their caravan back at the campsite, happy and content, a wicker picnic basket beside her and the radio playing quietly in the background. She loved to watch the activities going on around her, receiving great satisfaction from seeing so many people sharing so many wonderful moments together, moments that would be etched into their memories forever or captured by dozens of clicking cameras.

But, it was watching her husband that gave her the most pleasure, as he collaborated and played with the seagulls by the protecting sea wall. He sat there on the rugged rock formation, immersed in his own world, tossing bread crusts and slices of luncheon meat onto the warm sand that he had cheekily acquired from the picnic basket.

What seemed like a thousand calling birds congregating around him, all demanding to be fed, while many others elegantly and expertly patrolled the blue sky, like a squadron of fighter aircraft, assessing the commotion below them, either not hungry or too hesitant to join the feast. She could clearly see how much joy it bought him, his broad smile apparent as he threw nibbles high into the air, to be caught in mid-flight with perfect precision and judgement.

"Mrs Silva," a voice gently called her.

The seagulls continued to hop, skip and jump in the sand as they indulged in their feeding frenzy. They…

"Veronica," said the same soft voice.

She looked around the breathtaking view, to an orchestra of singing birds, but could see nobody addressing her. Her husband was still working as the waiter to the gulls, as they perched patiently at their tables, knives and forks in claws, waiting for their meals to arrive.

Veronica's body began to rock gently from side to side. Was she now on a boat, swaying to and fro with the swelling of the sea or swinging to the relaxing tunes from the radio?

"Mrs Silva," came the friendly female voice. "Wake up. Time to wake up now."

She slowly began to return to consciousness, desperately trying to cling on to her dream, not wanting to let it go. The wondrous, special moments that her mind had recalled fragmented and then dissipated.

Her eyes opened to the figure of Lisa, lightly shaking her and speaking her name and, as her vision adjusted to the dim lightening, three more people standing nearby, two men and a lady.

"Hi, hi," Lisa said with a comforting smile. "I'm glad you managed to sleep," she told her. "You've been out for over two hours."

Veronica sheepishly sat up, rubbing the hardened sleep from her eyes. "What time is it?"

Lisa glanced at her watch, a gold piece with a thin, delicate looking strap. "It's half-past three," she answered. She stepped aside and opened her palms to the strangers behind her. "Veronica, this is Doctor Nathan." The doctor nodded his head and smiled. "He is going to give you a checkup and talk with you awhile. And this is Livia Macedo," she said, pointing to the well-dressed lady in a black suit. "She is a countryman of yours from the Brazilian embassy. She's an interpreter."

Lisa nodded her head. "I know, I know. I realise that your English is OK, but this is standard procedure. She will interpret any ongoing conversation if there is anything you don't quite understand. It's just protocol," she explained. "And this is Mark Jones. He is a Family Liaison Officer."

Mr Jones approached the sofa. "Hello, Veronica," he greeted. "How are you feeling?"

"Do you have any news about my husband?"

Before sitting next to her on the sofa, he glanced at Lisa. "Veronica, you need to prepare yourself," he advised her. "I'm so sorry to have to tell you this, but your husband is dead." He paused before telling her that Mr Sergio Alveraz was also dead.

She looked up at the ceiling, nodding, taking a long deep breath. It was the news that she had been expecting, as she knew there was no real possibility of him surviving. In the early hours of this morning, she may have been in denial for a while but she sensed that he had had very little chance. A light tear formed on her eyelid, dropping onto the jumpsuit and then another. She didn't cry as she might have but the steady stream of dripping tears was enough. Her biggest fears had just been confirmed and the process of grieving could begin.

After the officer had finished speaking, Miss Macedo translated his statement in to perfect Portuguese but Veronica didn't need her to as she understood exactly what was said.

The standard procedure of crying may not have begun yet but here, sitting on a sofa in the safety of a police station, sat a devastated human being, in a foreign land, in a monstrous, unbearable and extremely painful situation. A woman that had no strength, no voice, no family and no real reason to live. A woman that yesterday had everything and today, nothing. All cruelly taken away from her, in a blink of an eye.

Veronica spent two hours talking with Dr Jones, asking her a long series of endless questions, occasionally referring to forms attached to a clipboard on his lap. Every now and then, he would write a note in the margins, before flicking the page over and moving on to the next one. She assumed that he was assessing her current state of mind and whether she might be a threat to herself or anyone else. A tray of food was bought in, a bowl of soup together with a cup of coffee and a glass of water, but she had no interest in eating, even though she knew she should. The only thing she wanted was for her husband to be by her side again.

At the end of the session, the doctor assured the police that she was OK, considering the circumstances and that she was reacting normally to a very traumatic set of experiences. Based on the doctor's ruling, she was transferred to a police safe house, where the collection of evidence would commence. Amy, Lisa and Miss Macedo were all there, together with three police officers who, Veronica assumed, were leading the investigation. All interviews, chats and conversions were recorded as they built their case.

Veronica noticed that many of the questions were repeatedly asked but reworded in different ways. She assumed it was a tactical ploy, used to corroborate her answers. Miss Macedo was prominent every step of the way during questioning, translating when it was required. Lisa and Amy sat in the background, looking on but available to Veronica, should she need them.

In the long, drawn-out process, Veronica regularly asked to take a break to step away from it all for a while. Recalling all the upsetting details became too much for her sometimes but, for every minute that they did talk, it became just a tiny bit easier. Retelling the story over and over would cause her to cry, overcome with emotion and finding herself falling into a deep, bottomless void, from which there was no escape.

"Try to be strong, Veronica," Amy told her. "We all sympathise with you and how you are feeling but, in order for you to get justice, we need to complete these tasks."

"I know," she agreed. "I am fighting a formidable foe and sometimes I lose out, but my thirst for justice is so intense it wouldn't fit in the ocean. I want to see this maniac get what he deserves." She licked her mouth in an attempt to moisten her dry lips. "I was wondering if I could call my family in Brazil."

"Of course, you can."

The phone was answered by her sister Ines and, although she was overjoyed to hear her voice, she was unable to speak. Words refused to form on her lips. She passed the receiver to Miss Macedo, asking her to take the call and speak for her.

The phone call lasted fifteen minutes and Veronica thanked her for not just her help, but also her sensitivity.

Amy walked over and sat beside her at the table. "Veronica, we are going to put you in the care of the Tavio family," she explained. "You know them already, right? They work with you at the meat factory." Veronica acknowledged who they were. "They offered their spare room for you to use. We feel that it would be a good thing if you were in familiar surroundings, with people that speak your language." She waited for a reply but Veronica seemed preoccupied. "We'll do that sometime tomorrow. Are you OK with that?"

She looked up with a forced, unconvincing smile and nodded.

Veronica was moved from the safe house to the Tavio residence the following afternoon. The gathering of evidence and her various statements had been concluded by mid-morning, having worked together for the majority of the night. A couple of times she had tried to sleep, but it denied her.

She would just lay there, constantly thinking, wondering and regretting. The officers were very accommodating and sensitive to her predicament and were happy to continue the work, no matter what the time might be. Breakfast was cooked by Miss Macedo for them all, but Veronica ate nothing. A glass of water was all that her body wanted. Her lack of food consumption prompted the police doctor to prescribe her a liquid supplement for the time being and a mix of sleeping pills and antidepressants.

Despite her emotional fragility and toxicity, she was desperate to see the bodies of her husband and her good friend Sergio. She put in an official request to view them but it was categorically refused, for a number of reasons, the main one being that they were still being prepared for the purpose of evidence. The doctor also considered her as too emotionally unstable and would almost certainly make things worse. A formal identification would take place at some point, but only at the right time.

Before her arrival, Mr Tavio was advised to make her room as bare and as basic as possible, leaving just a few pieces of furniture, as certain items could trigger a panic attack. An item as simple as a soft toy, usually associated as being cute, cuddly, with a source of security and belonging, could potentially set off an episode of anxiety, as well as an everyday knock at the door.

With their choice of taking her in, came a heavy responsibility. They needed to constantly think long and hard about anything that may upset her, no matter how small or how trivial it may be. By taking Veronica under their wing, they were contracting themselves into looking after her, no matter what. She had retreated deep into her shell, away from everyday life and could only be coaxed back out very slowly and only when *she* was ready.

A few days later, still heavily depressed and still locked in her own self built prison, her two daughters, Ana Beatriz and Luciana, arrived in Bristol. Veronica had known for three days of their pending arrival, filling her heart with excitement and a resounding feeling of hope. It had been over two years since she'd seen any of her daughters and it was a real boost to her confidence and well-being. Having been given the all clear by the police to visit her, they arrived at her temporary home. They all shared a tight group hug, as well as sharing tears of joy and happiness.

"Oh, mum," Luciana commented. "We've been so worried about you. It's wonderful to see you again."

"You too," she concurred. "The both of you. You don't know what it means to me to have you both here."

"Mother, you look like you haven't slept for a week," Ana Beatriz observed. "You need to come back with us to Brazil."

She shook her head. "I can't do that, I'm afraid. There is an ongoing murder investigation and I am the only witness to it all," Veronica explained. "As I understand it, the police are trying to trace and find Sergio's family in Mozambique. Also, before Romulo's body can be repatriated, there has to be a formal identification." She spoke with so much pain and sadness. "I can't believe you are here. How long are you staying for?"

"I'm sorry, mum," Luciana said. "I can only stay for a week. I have work commitments back home. But Ana Beatriz will be here longer."

"That's right, mother. I am here for three weeks," Ana Beatriz promised. "Maybe longer if needed."

"That's nice to hear. Where are you staying?"

"To be honest, we hadn't thought that far ahead. We were hoping that you might help us."

"I'm sure it will be OK for you to stay here. Mrs Tavio has been very good to me since this all happened," Veronica said. "Everyone has, especially the police."

"What happened, mother?" Ana Beatriz enquired. "Do you want to talk about it?"

Veronica pondered over her question for a short while. She had already been over it a dozen times recently with the police and she didn't really want to go through it all again. It had become far too repetitive and she never did like a stuck record. "I'll tell you all about it, another day," she answered.

"What happened to your foot?" Luciana asked.

She looked down at the light bandaging, lifting her foot slightly. "Hmm, I found myself outside with no shoes on for a while. Luckily, it's going to be fine," she said. "How are you finding the snow outside?"

"I love it, mum," Luciana beamed. "It's so much fun but I hate the cold!"

Veronica raised a smile, her first genuine smile for some time. "Well," she said. "It would be just boring old rain without the cold and you can get the rain at home."

A light knock sounded on the bedroom door. "Yes," Veronica called.

Mrs Tavio opened the door. "Sorry to disturb you, Veronica," she said, standing in the doorway. "I was wondering if you would all like dinner."

"Thank you, Mrs Tavio. That's very kind," Veronica said appreciatively. "Can I ask if it's OK for my girls to sleep here during their stay? One will be here a week and the other around three weeks," she explained. "Would that be OK?"

Mrs Tavio gave it just a second thought. "Yes, yes," she replied. "That's fine. One can sleep on the sofa and we have a foldout bed in the garage. I'll get my husband to pull it out."

"Thank you so much," Veronica said. "For everything."

She smiled as she gently closed the door.

"Listen, girls," Veronica continued. "I'm not going to be much fun, I'm afraid. I don't want to go out anywhere right now so, if you want to see Bristol, you'll have to make your own entertainment."

"It's fine, mum," Luciana said. "We didn't come all this way to sightsee. We came all this way to be with you."

"It's OK, Mrs Silva. Don't be frightened."

Veronica heard his words but, as she stood in front of the table, they meant very little. He was a short man, perhaps only five feet or so, well dressed in a grey suit and a matching tie, partially hidden by his oversized white medical coat. His moustache was in dire need of trimming. Standing next to him was Miss Macedo and, in the background close to the door, were Lisa and Ana Beatriz, silently watching on.

Against the wall of the small, rectangular room were four long rows of freezers, stacked on top of each other, some with a white name tag hanging from their door handles. Two of the freezer doors were open. On the vast sized table lay two bodies, covered in thin white sheets, hugging their contours closely, easily revealing their identities.

The coroner removed the plastic binder from underneath his arm, holding it in his hand. "Are you ready?" he said slowly and clearly.

She took a sharp intake of breath and quickly nodded her head.

He stepped forward and gently lifted the corner of the sheet, exposing Sergio's static face. Veronica bravely looked down at his closed eyes, his mouth also closed and his hair brushed and neatly tidied. His skin looked pale and spectral, like a bit part actor's make-up in a horror movie. The two neck wounds had been cleaned and stitched up and on the side of his face, a six-inch gash snaked from his ear to his jaw.

She stood motionless and ashen-faced, her heart full of sorrow, sadness and pain and her head full of anger, fury and hatred. Her vision began to blur as a tear formed in her eye, nestling into her bottom eyelid. She wiped it away with the sleeve of her sweater.

The coroner lightly placed a hand on her shoulder. "Is this Sergio Alveraz, Mrs Silva?" he asked.

"Yes," she replied, nodding her head. "Yes—It's him."

He opened the binder in his hand, removed a pen from his top pocket and made a few notes, before closing it again with the pen inside. He took a couple of steps down the table and lifted the second sheet. "Is this Romulo Silva, Veronica?"

She looked blankly at him as he lay lifeless before her. There were no visible injuries on his face, no cuts, no bruises and no lacerations; still looking so handsome, even in death. Her tears flowed freely, falling to the floor after bouncing from her shoes. She looked for a minute before turning to the coroner. "Yes," she sobbed. "This is Romulo."

He wrote down more notes before tucking his pen back into his pocket. "Thank you, Mrs Silva. Would you like a minute on your own?"

"Can I see the injuries to his chest?" she requested, to her continuous crying sobs.

He shook his head. "We just needed you to identify them. You shouldn't put yourself through more unnecessary pain."

"Please. Let me see."

The coroner briefly hesitated. "OK, it's your right to do so."

He peeled back the sheet to the bottom of his stomach, exposing six stab wounds, two to his chest and four to his abdomen.

Veronica shook her head in disbelief. What could possibly warrant such a frenzied attack on such a gentle, likeable and lovable man? A man that always put himself second behind those around him and a man whose charitable heart would never let his friends and family down.

The coroner left her in her own private thoughts for a few moments before replacing the sheet. "He received seven stab wounds, six at the front and one on his back," he explained, trying to remain tactful and sensitive to her feelings. "We're pretty sure that the wound on his back was the first. The rest were inflicted as he tried to defend himself. None of them were immediately fatal. The cause of death on his certificate will be listed as excessive blood loss due to the knife wounds."

Veronica repeated his words in her mind, as if she were trying to comprehend and understand their meaning. She took a few deep breaths, trying to combat the nausea building in her stomach. Again, she wiped her eyes and nose on her sweater. "Can I have that moment you offered?"

"Of course," he said, gesturing to the others to leave. "We'll wait for you outside."

She touched the side of his face with her finger, running it down his cheek. It felt icy cold to the touch. "I promise you, here and now," she whispered. "That this monster will not go unpunished. I will not rest until you have justice for the destruction of our lives and our happiness."

Her heart sank as she remembered her father's words. "Oh, my darling. Look what has happened to the ferocious, fearless lion. Why couldn't you have been the mangy old dog that I so terribly wanted you to be?" She placed her palm on his scalp, bent down and kissed him gently on the cheek. "Goodbye, my love. One day, I will join you and our love will be served."

Chapter Ten

Romulo's body was finally repatriated from Bristol, England, back to Portugal on 17 February 2003, six weeks after his brutal murder. His funeral took place two days later at his place of birth in Sintra, West Lisbon, on the Portuguese Riviera. There were over one hundred mourners. Despite her fragile age and deteriorating health, his mother attended the ceremony but his father, too old and too frail, was unable to go. Also in attendance were Veronica and her eldest daughter, Ana Beatriz.

After extensive investigations and inquiries, Sergio Alveraz's family were never traced nor found in Mozambique. He was cremated in Bristol, England on 21 February 2003. There were just two attendees; Veronica and his ever loving fiancée, Claire. Veronica's son, Junior, disappeared in 2001 without a trace and none of her family have seen nor heard from him since. The last that she heard was that he no longer lived with his father.

Her brother-in-law, who so brutally raped her on her fifteenth birthday, was never questioned, arrested, tried or convicted of his crime. A number of years later, she discovered that he had lost his sight and gone blind and was living in a care home where he had no visitors, rejected by society and banished to live his life—alone.

Over a period of five weeks, there were four hearings at Bristol Crown Court, all carefully shadowed by Veronica. At the first hearing, Alfonso remained completely silent, in total defiance, not even confirming his own name. It was as if he refused to recognise the jurisdiction of the court. However, on the third hearing, he pleaded guilty to two counts of murder in the first degree and one count of attempted murder.

On 14 March 2003, he was sentenced to twenty-six years in prison with no parole and, in 2029, to be released into the care of a psychiatric hospital, never to be allowed back into society again. The justice that Veronica had so vehemently fought for came to fruition and, knowing that Alfonso could never hurt anyone again, gave Romulo the peace that he so very much deserved.

It took eighteen months for Veronica to recover from Panic Disorder, with regular hospital appointments and endless counselling sessions. The two lengthy scars on her hand remain, permanently embedded, a constant reminder of her horrific ordeal but the scars in her memory had already begun to decline and fade.

In August 2005, she returned to Brazil to arrange the emigration of her family, with her three daughters now living with her in England. Over time, her daughters have proudly given her four wonderful grandchildren and enjoy spending endless days with them. Six years after Romulo's death, she remarried and now leads a fulfilling, happy, joyous life. She is most content when tending the flowers in their garden with her husband.

However, whenever she admires a seagull elegantly riding the breeze, whether from her bedroom window or on a day trip to the coast, it always reminds her of her dear departed husband.

THE END